CHARLES SPURGEON

~ *Christian Living Classics* ~

What the Holy Spirit Does in a Believer's Life

~ Compiled and Edited by ROBERT HALL ~

Emerald Books

P.O. Box 635 • Lynnwood, Washington 98046

Scripture quotations are taken from the King James Version of the Bible.

WHAT THE HOLY SPIRIT DOES IN A BELIEVER'S LIFE
Copyright © 1993
Lance C. Wubbels
All Rights Reserved

ISBN 1-883002-01-X

Published by Emerald Books
P.O. box 635
Lynnwood, Washington 98046

Printed in the United States of America

To My Wife

Karen

"Many women have done excellently, but you
surpass them all."

CHARLES SPURGEON
CHRISTIAN LIVING CLASSICS

Grace Abounding in a Believer's Life

A Passion for Holiness in a Believer's Life

The Power of Christ's Miracles

The Power of the Cross of Christ

The Power of Prayer in a Believer's Life

Spiritual Warfare in a Believer's Life

The Triumph of Faith in a Believer's Life

What the Holy Spirit Does in a Believer's Life

The Power of Christ's Miracles

F.B. MEYER
CHRISTIAN LIVING CLASSICS

Paul: A Servant of Jesus Christ

David: Shepherd, Psalmist, King

Joseph: Beloved Hated, and Exalted

Abraham: The Obedience of Faith

Moses: Servant of God

Peter: Fisherman, Disciple, Apostle

About the Editor

ROBERT HALL is the pseudonym for Lance Wubbels, the managing editor of Bethany House Publishers. His interest in the writings of Charles Spurgeon began while doing research on an editorial project that required extensive reading of Spurgeon's sermons. He discovered a wealth of sermon classics that are filled with practical, biblical insight for every believer and written in a timeless manner that makes them as relevant today as the day they were spoken. His desire is to select and present Spurgeon's writings in a way that will appeal to a wide audience of readers and allow one of the greatest preachers of all time to enrich believers' lives.

About the Author

CHARLES HADDON SPURGEON (1834–1892) was the remarkable British "Boy Preacher of the Fens" who became one of the truly greatest preachers of all time. Coming from a flourishing country pastorate in 1854, he accepted a call to pastor London's New Park Street Chapel. This building soon proved too small and so work on Spurgeon's Metropolitan Tabernacle was begun in 1859. Meanwhile his weekly sermons were being printed and having a remarkable sale—25,000 copies every week in 1865 and translated into more than twenty languages.

Spurgeon built the Metropolitan Tabernacle into a congregation of over 6,000 and added well over 14,000 members during his thirty-eight-year London ministry. The combination of his clear voice, his mastery of language, his sure grasp of Scripture, and a deep love for Christ produced some of the noblest preaching of any age. An astounding 3,561 sermons have been preserved in sixty-three volumes, *The New Park Street Pulpit* and *The Metropolitan Tabernacle Pulpit*, from which the chapters of this book have been selected and edited.

During his lifetime, Spurgeon is estimated to have preached to 10,000,000 people. He remains history's most widely read preacher. There is more available material written by Spurgeon than by any other Christian author, living or dead. His sixty-three volumes of sermons stand as the largest set of books by a single author in the history of Christianity, comprising the equivalent to the twenty-seven volumes of the ninth edition of the *Encyclopedia Britannica*.

Contents

Introduction

NO PERIOD IN THE LIFE of the church of
Jesus Christ has ever been without its own set of doctrinal controversies. Some controversies involved the championing of
monumental issues that kept the church from falling into heresy—such as Athanasius contesting Arius and the Arians during
most of the fourth century. Other controversies have regarded
such trivialities and been so ludicrous that we might consider
them humorous except for the divisiveness that they engendered
within the church.

One of the controversies of our day surrounds the person
and the work of the Holy Spirit in the life of the church and the
lives of believers. There are those within the church who emphatically proclaim that if the Holy Spirit is present in His fullness within a church, signs and wonders will be commonplace.
Others say that the Holy Spirit is restoring the New Testament
roles of apostles and prophets for today's church. Some believers
claim the greatest work of the Holy Spirit is His sanctifying
power and seem preoccupied with personal holiness. Still others
redefine the Holy Spirit's role in sanctification, and then state
that the true role of the Holy Spirit regards the empowering of
the believer for proclaiming the gospel and the fulfilment of the
Great Commission.

Confusing, isn't it. The winds of doctrine blow in every direction imaginable.

While this book does not attempt to solve the controversies,
my hope is that it will help bring a sound biblical balance to the
lives of believers. If we are to be like the people the Apostle Paul

described when he said, "no longer be infants, tossed back and forth by the waves, and blown here and there by every wind of teaching" (Ephesians 4:14), it must involve receiving a firm foundation on the basic truths regarding the Holy Spirit. While we need not hope to establish a dogmatic teaching that resolves every issue, we are justified in believing that Scripture contains the pillars necessary for us to understand the person and work of the Holy Spirit as well as truly live a Spirit-filled life consistent with that seen in the Bible.

As one of the greatest expository preachers of all time, Charles Spurgeon is eminently qualified to teach on the Holy Spirit. His amazing thirty-eight-year metropolitan ministry in the city of London during the 1800s marked an era of some of the most gifted pastors ever assembled in Great Britain—Joseph Parker, H.P. Liddon, Hugh Price Hughes, F.B. Meyers, R.W. Dale, Alexander Maclaren, Alexander Whyte, F.W. Farrar. But in the matter of influence for the gospel—both in large audiences and through the printed page—none matched Spurgeon's contribution. His ministry was said to have been a success unparalleled in England since the days of Whitefield and Wesley.

Charles Spurgeon credited his success to the powerful work of the Holy Spirit. He firmly believed that the spiritual transformations that occurred throughout the book of Acts were only the beginning of the mighty works the Holy Spirit intends to do. He stressed over and over that nothing about the Holy Spirit has diminished since Pentecost; indeed, he felt that Pentecost was not the pinnacle of the church's experience but only the first unveiling of what could and should happen. He called to the church to receive and live up to the full potential of the Holy Spirit.

I invite you to read these twelve marvelous chapters as you would listen to a trusted and skilled pastor. Spurgeon's teaching is so solidly biblical, so understandable, so passionate, so wonderfully visual, and so practical that one cannot help but be inspired and challenged. Life-changing messages on the person and work of the Holy Spirit await you.

Billy Graham has said: "There is something authentic and timeless about Spurgeon's sermons. Through them he speaks to our generation, as he did to his own, of the unchanging truth of

Christ. I commend them to modern man as an example of the perennial power of the Word of God as it speaks to man in his need."

Careful editing to these sermons that were given well over one hundred years ago help sharpen their focus while retaining the authentic and timeless flavor they undoubtedly bring.

*W*ind and fire! Rushing mighty wind alone how terrible! Who shall stand against it? See how the gallant ships dash together and the monarchs of the forest bow their heads. And fire alone! Who shall stand against it when it devours its prey? But set wind and fire to work in hearty union! Remember the old city of London. When the flames first began, it was utterly impossible to quench them because the wind fanned the flame and the buildings gave way before the fire-torrent. And what a sight the forest is ablaze! Hear the mighty trees crashing in the flame! What can stand against it! The fire sets the mountains ablaze. What a smoke blackens the skies; the sky grows dark at noon. As hill after hill offers up its sacrifice, the timid imagine that the great day of the Lord has come. To see a spiritual blaze of equal grandeur would be the fulfilment of a devout wish. O God, send us the Holy Ghost in this manner. Give us both the breath of spiritual life and the fire of unconquerable zeal, till nation after nation shall yield to the sway of Jesus. Answer us both by wind and by fire, and then shall we see You to be God indeed.

Chapter One

The Pentecostal Wind and Fire

And suddenly there came a sound from heaven as of a rushing mighty wind, and it filled all the house where they were sitting. And there appeared unto them cloven tongues like as of fire, and it sat upon each of them. And they were all filled with the Holy Ghost, and began to speak with other tongues, as the Spirit gave them utterance—Acts 2:3–4.

THE DESCENT OF THE HOLY GHOST at Pentecost is the biblical model for what we may expect of His working in the church at the present time. Keep in mind that whatever the Holy Spirit was at the beginning He is now, for as God He cannot change. Correspondingly, whatever He did then He is able to do still, for His power is by no means diminished. As the prophet Micah stated, "O thou that art named the house of Jacob, is the spirit of the Lord straitened?" (Mic. 2:7). We greatly grieve the Holy Spirit if we suppose that His might is less today than in the beginning. Although we may not expect—and need not desire—the literal, physical manifestations that came with the gift of the Holy Spirit, yet we may both desire and expect that which was intended and symbolized by them; and we may expect to see the same spiritual wonders performed among us today.

Pentecost, according to the belief of the Jews, was the time of the giving of the law. If when the law was given there was a marvelous display of power on Sinai, it was to be expected that when the gospel was given, whose declaration is far more glorious, there should be some special unveiling of the divine presence. If at the commencement of the gospel we see the Holy Spirit working great signs and wonders, may we not expect a continuance—if anything, an increased display—of His power as the ages roll on? The law vanished, but the gospel will never vanish; it shines brighter and brighter to the perfect millennial day. It should not be forgotten that Pentecost was the feast of first fruits, the time when the first ears of ripe corn were offered to God. If, then, at the commencement of the gospel harvest we see so plainly the power of the Holy Spirit, may we not most properly expect infinitely more as the harvest advances, and most of all when the greatest harvest is ready to be gathered? May we not conclude that if Pentecost was thus marvelous, the actual harvest will be more wonderful still?

Pentecost should be viewed not as a piece of history but as a fact of great relevance for us today. The Father sent us the Comforter that He may dwell in us till the coming of the Lord. The Holy Spirit has never returned, for He came in accordance with the Savior's prayer to abide with us forever. The gift of the Comforter was not temporary, and the display of His power was not to be once seen and seen no more. The Holy Ghost is here, and we should expect His divine working among us today just as at Pentecost. If that is not our experience, we should search ourselves to see what it is that hinders, whether it is something in our lives that grieves Him or restrains His sacred energy. May God increase our faith in the Holy Spirit and inflame our desires toward Him so that we may look to see Him fulfilling His mission among men as at the beginning.

The Instructive Symbols of the Holy Spirit

There were two prominent symbols of the Holy Spirit at Pentecost: a sound as of a rushing mighty wind and cloven tongues as it were of fire.

Take the symbols separately. The first is *wind*—an emblem of deity and therefore a proper symbol of the Holy Spirit. Throughout the Old Testament, God revealed Himself under the emblem of breath or wind: indeed, the Hebrew word for "wind" and "spirit" is the same. So with the Greek word, when Christ spoke to Nicodemus, it is difficult for translators to tell us when He said "spirit" and when He said "wind." Indeed, some most correctly render the original all the way through by the word *wind*, while others with much reason have used the word *spirit*. The original word signified either the one or the other, or both. Wind is, of all material things, one of the most spiritual in appearance; it is invisible, ethereal, mysterious. Consequently, men have fixed upon it as being nearest akin to spirit. In Ezekiel's famous vision of the valley full of dry bones, it is clear that the Spirit of God was intended by that vivifying wind that came when the prophet prophesied and blew upon the withered relics till they were quickened into life. "The Lord hath his way in the whirlwind" (Nahum 1:3); thus He displays Himself when He works. "The Lord answered Job out of the whirlwind" (Job 38:1); thus He reveals Himself when He teaches His servants.

Observe that this wind was on the day of Pentecost accompanied with a sound as of rushing mighty wind, for while the Spirit of God can work in silence, He frequently uses sound. I would be the last to depreciate meetings in which there is nothing but holy silence, for I could wish that we had more reverence for silence, and it is in stillness that the inner life is nourished. Yet the Holy Ghost does not work for the advancement of the kingdom of God by silence alone, for faith comes by hearing. If the Lord had not given men ears or tongues, silent worship would have been not only appropriate but also necessary; but inasmuch as we have ears, the Lord must have intended us to hear something, and as we have tongues, He must have meant us to speak. Some of us would be glad to be silent, but where the gospel has free course, there is sure to be a measure of noise and stir. The sound came on this occasion, no doubt, to call the attention of the assembly to what was about to occur, to arouse them, and to fill them with awe! There is something indescribably solemn about the rush of a rising tempest; it bows the soul before the sublime mystery of divine power. What more fitting as an attendant upon divine working than the deeply solemn rush of a mighty wind.

With this awe-inspiring sound as of a mighty wind, there was clear indication of the wind's coming from heaven. Ordinary winds blow from this or that direction, but this wind descended from heaven itself: it was distinctly like a downdraft from above. This sets forth the fact that the true Spirit comes from neither this place nor that, nor can His power be controlled or directed by human authority, but His working is ever from above, from God Himself. The work of the Holy Spirit is, so to speak, the breath of God, and His power is evermore in a special sense the immediate power of God. Coming downward, therefore, this mysterious wind passed into the house where the disciples were gathered and filled the room. An ordinary rushing mighty wind would probably have destroyed the house; but this heavenly gust filled but did not destroy, it blessed but did not overthrow the waiting company.

The meaning of the symbol is that as breath, air, wind, is the very life of man, so the Spirit of God is the life of the spiritual man. By Him we are reborn at the first; by Him our spiritual life is sustained; by Him is the inner life nurtured and increased and perfected. The breath of the nostrils of the man of God is the Spirit of God.

This holy breath was intended not only to quicken the disciples but also to invigorate them. How gladly we welcome a gust from the breezy down or a gale from the open sea! If the winds of earth are so refreshing, what must a wind from heaven be! That rushing mighty wind soon cleared away all earthly staleness. It aroused the disciples and left them prepared for the coming work of the Lord. The disciples took in great drafts of heavenly life; they felt animated, aroused, and stirred. A sacred enthusiasm came upon them because they were filled with the Holy Ghost, and endued with that strength, they rose into a nobler form of life than they had known before.

This wind demonstrated the irresistible power of the Holy Spirit, for simple as the air is, and mobile and apparently feeble, yet set it in motion, and you feel that a thing of life is among you. Increase that motion, and who knows the power of the restless giant who has been awakened. See, it becomes a storm, a tempest, a hurricane, a tornado. Nothing can be more potent than the wind when it is thoroughly aroused; and so, though the Spirit of God be despised among men, yet let Him work with the fullness of His power and you will see what He can do. He comes softly, breathing like a gentle zephyr that fans the flowers but does not dislodge the insect of most gauzy wing, and our hearts are comforted. He comes like a stirring breeze, and we are quickened to a livelier diligence: our sails are hoisted, and we fly before the gale. He comes with yet greater strength, and we prostrate ourselves in the dust as we hear the thunder of His power, bringing down with a crash false confidences and refuges of lies! How the firm reliances of carnal men, which seemed to stand like rocks, are utterly cast down! How men's hopes, which appeared to be rooted like oaks, are torn up by the roots before the breath of the convincing Spirit! What can stand against Him? Oh, that we did see something of that mighty rushing wind that breaks the cedars of Lebanon and sweeps before it all that resist its power!

The second Pentecostal symbol was *fire*—also a frequent symbol of deity. Abraham saw a burning lamp, and Moses beheld a burning bush. When Solomon had built his holy and beautiful house, the temple's consecration lay in the fire of God descending upon the sacrifice to mark that the Lord was there, for when the Lord before had dwelt in the tabernacle, He revealed Himself in a pillar of cloud by day and a pillar of fire by night. "Our God is a consuming fire" (Heb. 12:29). Hence the symbol of fire is a fit emblem of God the Holy Spirit. Let us adore and worship the Holy Spirit.

Tongues of flame sitting on each man's head indicate a personal visitation to the mind and heart of each one of the chosen company. Not to consume them came the fires, for no one was injured by the flaming tongue. To men whom the Lord has prepared for His approach, there is no danger in the Lord's visitations. Such men see God, and their lives are preserved; they feel God's fires and are not consumed. This is the exclusive privilege of those who have been prepared and purified for such fellowship with God.

The intention of the symbol was to show the disciples that the Holy Spirit would illuminate them as fire gives light. "He shall guide you into all truth" (John 16:13). Henceforth the disciples were to be no more children untrained but to be teachers in Israel, instructors of the nations whom they were to disciple for Christ. Hence, the Spirit of light was upon them. But fire does more than give light. It inflames, and the flames that sat upon each showed the disciples that they were to be ablaze with love, intense with zeal, burning with self-sacrifice, and that they were to go forth among men to speak not with the chill tongue of deliberate logic but with burning tongues of passionate pleading—persuading and entreating men to come to Christ that they might live. The fire signified inspiration. God was about to make the disciples speak under a divine influence, to speak as the Spirit of God should give them utterance. O blessed symbol, would to God that we experienced its full meaning and that the tongue of fire sat upon every servant of the Lord. May a fire burn steadily within to destroy our sin, a holy sacrificial flame to make us whole burnt offerings to God, a never-dying flame of zeal for God and devotion to the cross.

Note that the emblem was not just fire but a tongue of fire, for God meant to have a speaking church—not a church that would fight with the sword but a church that should have a sword proceeding out of its mouth, whose one weapon should be the proclamation of the gospel of Jesus Christ.

From what I know of some preachers, when they had their Pentecost, the influence sat upon them in the form of tongues of flowers; but the apostolic Pentecost knew only about flames. What fine preaching we have now! What new thoughts and poetical turns! This is not the style of the Holy Ghost. Soft and gentle is the flow of smooth speech that tells of the dignity of man, the grandeur of the century, the toning down of all punishment for sin, and the probable restoration of all lost spirits, including the archfiend himself. This is the Satanic ministry, subtle as the serpent, bland as his seducing words to Eve. The Holy Spirit does not call us to this mode of speech. Fire, intensity, zeal, passion as much as you will, but as for aiming at effect by polished phrases and brilliant periods—these are fitter for those who would deceive men than for those who declare the message of the Most High. The style of the Holy Ghost is one that conveys the truth to the mind in the most forcible manner—it is plain but flaming, simple but consuming. The Holy Spirit has never written a cold period throughout the whole Bible and has never spoken a lifeless word to a man, but evermore He gives and blesses the tongue of fire.

These—wind and fire—are the two symbols, and I should like you to carefully observe the Holy Spirit's instruction by them. When the Holy Spirit came from the Father to His Son Jesus, it was as a dove. Let peace rest on that dear Sufferer's soul through all His days of labor and through the passion that would close them. Jesus' anointing is that of peace: Jesus needed no tongue of flame, for He was already all on fire with love. When the Holy Spirit was bestowed by the Son of God upon His disciples, it was a Spirit breath—"He breathed on them, and saith unto them, Receive ye the Holy Ghost" (John 20:22).

To have life more abundantly is a chief necessity of servants of the Lord Jesus, and therefore the Holy Ghost visits us. Now that we have the Holy Spirit from Christ as our inner life, the Holy Spirit comes upon us with the intent to use us in blessing others, and this is the manner of His visitation—He comes as the wind that carries the words we speak, as fire that burns a way for the truth we utter. Our words are now full of life and flame; they are borne by the breath of the Spirit, and they fall like fire-flakes and set the souls of men blazing with desire after God. If the Holy Spirit shall rest upon us to qualify us for service, it shall be in this manner—not merely of life for ourselves but of fiery energy in dealing with others. Come on us even now, O rushing mighty wind and tongue of fire, for the world has great need. It lies stagnant in the malaria of sin and needs a healing wind. It is shrouded in dreadful night and needs the flaming torch of truth. There is neither health nor light for this world but from You, O blessed Spirit; come, then, upon it through Your people.

Now put these symbols together: wind and fire! Rushing mighty wind alone how terrible! Who shall stand against it? See how the gallant ships dash together and the monarchs of the forest bow their heads. And fire alone! Who shall stand against it when it devours its prey? But set wind and fire to work in hearty union! Remember the old city of London. When the flames first began, it was utterly impossible to quench them because the wind fanned the flame and the buildings gave way before the fire-torrent. And what a sight the forest is ablaze! Hear the mighty trees crashing in the flame! What can stand against it! The fire sets the mountains ablaze. What a smoke blackens the skies; the sky grows dark at noon. As hill after hill offers up its sacrifice, the timid imagine that the great day of the Lord has come. To see a spiritual blaze of equal grandeur would be the fulfilment of a devout wish. O God, send us the Holy Ghost in this manner. Give us both the breath of spiritual life and the fire of unconquerable zeal, till nation after nation shall yield to the sway of Jesus. Answer us both by wind and by fire, and then shall we see You to be God indeed. The kingdom comes not, and the work has lost its strength. Lord, bring us to this waiting place where we are all of one accord, all believing, all expecting, all prepared by prayer.

The Immediate Effects of Pentecost

The descent of the Holy Spirit was marked by two immediate effects: the first was *filling*, and the second was *the gift of utterance*. I call special attention to the first—namely, filling. The Holy Spirit did not merely fill the house; He filled the men—"they were all filled with the Holy Ghost." When the men stood up to speak, even the vulgar mockers in the crowd noticed this. They said, "These men are full"; and though they added "of new wine" (Acts 2:13), they evidently detected a singular fullness about them. We are poor, empty things by nature and useless while we remain so: we need to be filled with the Holy Ghost.

Unfortunately, some people read this verse and seem to believe in the Spirit of God giving utterance only, and they look upon instruction in divine things as of secondary importance. What trouble comes when that theory is acted upon! How the empty vessels clatter and rattle and sound! Men in such case utter a wonderful amount of nothing, and even when that nothing is set on fire, it does not come to much. I dread a revival of that sort, where the first thing and the last thing is everlasting talk. Those placed as teachers ought to be themselves taught of the Lord. How can they communicate what they have not received? Where the Spirit of God is truly at work, He first fills and then gives utterance: that is His way. Oh, that you and I were at this moment filled with the Holy Ghost!

"Full!" Then there was no room for anything else in any one of them! They were too completely occupied by the heavenly power to have room for the desires of the flesh. Fear was banished; every minor motive was expelled: the Spirit of God flooded their very being and drove out everything that was extraneous. The disciples had many faults and many weaknesses before they were filled with the Spirit of God; but on that day, faults and weaknesses were no longer perceptible. The disciples became different men from what they had ever been before: men full of God are the reverse of men full of self.

The difference between an empty man and a full man is something very wonderful. Let a thirsty man have an empty vessel handed to him. There may be much noise in the handling, but what a mockery it is as the vessel touches the man's lips. But fill the vessel with refreshing water, and perhaps there may be all the more silence in the passing it, for a full cup needs careful handling. But oh, what a blessing when the vessel reaches the man's lips! Out of a full vessel, the man may drink his full. Out of a full church, the world shall receive salvation, but never out of an empty one. The first thing we need as a church is to be filled with the Holy Ghost: the gift of utterance will then come as a matter of course. "Spring up, O well." If it is a fountain of living water, who would restrain it, who could restrain it? Let him overflow who is full, but be careful that he does not set up to pour out when there is nothing in him. If he counts it his official duty to go pouring out, pouring out, pouring out, at unreasonable length, and yet nothing comes of it, I am sure he acts, not by the Holy Spirit, but according to his own vanity.

The next Pentecostal symbol was *utterance*. As soon as the Spirit of God filled them, the disciples began to speak. It seems to me they actually began to speak before the people had come together. They could not help it; the inner forces demanded expression, and they had to speak. When the Spirit of God really comes upon a man, the man does not wait till he has gathered an audience of the size that he desires, but he seizes the next opportunity. He speaks to one person, he speaks to two, he speaks to three, to anyone: he must speak, for he is full.

When the Spirit of God fills a man, the man speaks so as to be understood. The crowd spoke different languages, and these Spirit-filled men spoke to the members of the crowd in the language of the country in which they were born. This is one of the signs of the Spirit's utterance. If an educated brother fires over the heads of his congregation with a grand oration, he may trace his elocution to Cicero and Demosthenes, but do not let him ascribe it to the Holy Spirit, for that is not the Holy Spirit's style. The Spirit speaks so that His words may be understood, and if there is obscurity, it lies in the language used by the Lord Himself.

The crowd not only understood but also felt. There were lancets in this Pentecostal preaching, and the hearers "were pricked in the heart" (Acts 2:37). The truth wounded men, and the slain of the Lord were many, for the wounds were in the most vital part. The hearers could not understand it: they had heard speakers before, but this was different. The man spoke fire-flakes, and one hearer cried to his fellow, "What is this?" The preachers were a speaking flame, and the fire dropped into the hearts of men till the men were amazed and confounded.

Thus are the two effects of the Holy Spirit: a fullness of the Spirit in the ministry and the church, and a fire ministry and a church on fire, speaking so as to be felt and understood by those around. Causes produce effects like themselves, and this wind and fire ministry soon did its work. We read that "this was noised abroad" (Acts 2:6). Of course it was, because there had been a noise as of a rushing mighty wind. Next to that we read that all the people came together and were confounded. There was naturally a stir, for a great wind from heaven was rushing. All were amazed and astonished, and while some inquired believingly, others began to mock. Of course they did: there was a fire burning, and fire is a dividing thing; and this fire began to separate between the precious and the vile, as fire always will do when it comes into operation. We may expect at the beginning of a true revival to observe a movement among the people, a noise, and a stir. These things are not done in a corner. Cities will know of the presence of God, and crowds will be attracted by the event.

The Primary Message of the Holy Spirit

With the Holy Spirit being so evidently at work, what was the most prominent subject that these full men began to preach about with words of fire? Suppose that the Holy Spirit should work mightily in the church today. What would our ministers preach about? Predestination and free agency? I do not think so: these would happily be ended, for they tend toward bitterness. Would we hear a great deal about the premillennial and the post-millennial advent? I do not think so. I never saw much of the Spirit of God in discussions or dreamings upon times and seasons that are not clearly revealed. Should we hear learned essays upon advanced theology? No, sir. When the devil inspires the church, we have modern theology, but when the Spirit of God is among us, that rubbish is shot out with loathing.

What did these men preach about? Their hearers said, "We do hear them speak in our tongues the wonderful works of God" (Acts 2:11). Oh, that this might be to my dying day my sole topic—the wonderful works of God! First the disciples spoke of *redemption*—that wonderful work of God. Peter's sermon exemplifies how they spoke. Peter told the people that Jesus was the Son of God, that the people had crucified and slain Him, but that He had come to redeem men and that there was salvation through His precious blood. Peter preached redemption. How this land will echo again and again with "Redemption, redemption, redemption, redemption by the precious blood," when the Holy Ghost is among us. This is fit fuel for the tongue of flame— something worthy to be blown about by the divine wind. This is one of the wonderful works of God of which we can never make too frequent mention.

The disciples certainly spoke of the next wonderful work of God—*regeneration.* There was no concealing the work of the Holy Spirit in that ministry of Pentecost. Peter said, "Ye shall receive the gift of the Holy Ghost" (Acts 2:38). The preachers of Pentecost told of the Spirit's work by the Spirit's power: conversion, repentance, renewal, faith, and holiness were freely spoken of and ascribed to their real author—the divine Spirit. When the Spirit of God gives a full and fiery ministry, we can expect to hear it clearly proclaimed, "Ye must be born again"; and we will see a people born not of blood or of the will of the flesh but of the will of God and by the energy that comes from heaven. A Holy Ghost ministry cannot be silent about the Holy Ghost and His sacred operations upon the heart.

Very plainly the disciples spoke of a third wonderful work of God—*the remission of sin.* This was the point that Peter pushed home to the hearers—that on repentance they should receive remission of sins. What a blessed message: pardon of crimes of deepest dye, a pardon bought with Jesus' blood, free pardon, full pardon, irreversible pardon given to the vilest of the vile when they ground their weapons of rebellion and bow at the feet that once were nailed to the tree. The divine message of fatherly forgiveness to returning prodigals is proof of a divine influence within the church.

These are the doctrines that the Holy Ghost will revive in the midst of the land when He works mightily: redemption, regeneration, remission. If you would have the Spirit of God resting on your labors, keep these three things ever to the front and make all men hear in their own tongue the wonderful works of God.

The Glorious Results of Pentecost

The first result of the Spirit's coming as wind and fire—filling and giving utterance—was a *deep feeling* in the hearers. There was never, perhaps, in the world such a feeling excited by the language of mortal man as that which was aroused in the crowds in Jerusalem on that day. We are told that those who listened were pricked in the heart. These people had painful emotions; they felt wounds that killed their enmity. The word struck at the center of their being: it pierced the vital point. Unfortunately, people come into our places of worship today to hear the preacher, and their friends ask them on their return, "How did you like him?" Was that the reason for going—to see how you liked him? Are preachers placed in the church as opportunities for criticism or entertainment?

O my reader, if preachers are true to our God and true to

you, theirs is a more solemn business than most men dream. The object of all true preaching is the heart—divorcing the heart from sin and wedding it to Christ. The ministry has failed and remains without the divine seal upon it unless it makes men tremble, makes them sad, and then brings them to Christ and causes them to rejoice.

Sermons are heard by the thousands, and yet how little comes of them all because the heart is not aimed at, or else the archers miss the mark. Alas, hearers do not present their hearts as the target but leave them at home and bring only their ears or their heads! Here we need the Almighty's aid. Pray powerfully that the Spirit of God may rest upon all who speak in God's name, for then they will create deep feeling in their hearers!

Then followed an *earnest inquiry*. "They were pricked in their heart, and said unto Peter and to the rest of the apostles, Men and brethren, what shall we do?" (Acts 2:37). Emotion is of itself but a poor result unless it leads to practical action. It must be a feeling that impels one to immediate movement or at least to earnest inquiry as to what one shall do. O Spirit of God, if You will rest on me, even me, men shall not hear and go their way and forget what they have heard! They will arise and seek the Father and taste His love. If You would rest on those who publish Your word, men would not merely weep while they hear, but they would go their way to ask, "What must we do to be saved?" This is what we need. We do not require new preachers; we need a new anointing of the Spirit. We do not require novel forms of service; we must have the fire Spirit, the wind Spirit, to work by us till people everywhere cry out for salvation.

Then came *a grand reception of the word*. We are told that the hearers gladly received the word, and they received it in two senses. First, Peter told them to repent, and they did. They were pricked to the heart on account of what they had done to Jesus, and they sorrowed after a godly manner and stopped their sins. They also believed on Him whom they had slain and accepted Him as their Savior without hesitancy. They trusted in Him whom God had set forth to be a propitiation, and thus they fully received the word. Repentance and faith make up a complete reception of Christ, and they had both. Why should we not see this divine result today?

But what next? They were *baptized* directly. Having repented and believed, the next step was to make confession of their faith. They did not postpone that act for a single day. Why should they? Willing hands were there, the whole company of the faithful were all glad to engage in the holy service, and that same day they were baptized. If the Holy Ghost were fully with us, we would never have to complain that many believers never confess their faith, for they would be eager to do so. Backwardness to be baptized comes too often from the fear of persecution, indecision, love of ease, pride, or disobedience; all these vanish when the heavenly wind and fire are doing their sacred work. Sinful diffidence soon disappears, sinful shame of Jesus is no more seen, and hesitancy and delay are banished forever when the Holy Spirit works with power.

Furthermore, as a result of the Spirit of God, there was *great steadfastness*. "They continued stedfastly in the apostles' doctrine" (Acts 2:42). We have had plenty of revivals of the human kind, and the results have been sadly disappointing. Excited, nominal converts have been multiplied: but where are they after a little testing? I am sad to say that there has been much sown and very little reaped that was worth reaping. Our hopes were flattering as a dream; but the apparent result has vanished like a vision of the night. But where the Spirit of God is really at work, the converts stand fast in the apostolic truth.

We see next that there was *abundant worship of God*, for the new converts were steadfast not only in the doctrine but also in breaking of bread and in prayer and in fellowship. There was no difficulty in getting a prayer meeting then, no difficulty in maintaining daily communion then, no lack of fellowship, for the Spirit of God was among them, and the ordinances were precious in their eyes. "Oh," say some, "if we could get this minister or that evangelist, we would be fine." Believers, if you had the Holy Spirit, you would have everything else growing out of His presence, for all good things are summed up in Him.

Next to this there came *striking generosity*. Funds were not hard to raise: liberality overflowed its banks, for believers poured all that they had into the common fund. Then was it seen to be true that the silver and gold are the Lord's. When the Spirit of God operates powerfully, there is little need to make strong appeals for the legitimate financial concerns of the church. There will be no lack of money when there is no lack of grace. When the Spirit of God comes, those who have substance yield it to their Lord: those who have but little grow rich by giving of that little, and those who are already rich become happy by consecrating what they have. There is no need to rattle the box when the rushing mighty wind is heard and the fire is dissolving all hearts in love.

Then came *continual gladness.* "They . . . did eat their meat with gladness" (Acts 2:46). They were not just glad at prayer meetings and sermons but were glad at breakfast and at supper. Whatever they had to eat, they were for singing over it. Jerusalem was the happiest city that ever was when the Spirit of God was there. The disciples were singing from morning to night, and I have no doubt the outsiders asked, "What is that all about?" The temple was never so frequented as then; there was never such singing before; the very streets of Jerusalem and the Hill of Zion rang with the once despised Galileans.

The disciples were full of gladness that showed itself in *praising God.* I have no doubt they broke out now and then in the services with shouts of "Glory! Hallelujah!" I think that all propriety was probably scattered to the winds. They were so glad, so exhilarated that they were ready to leap for joy. By way of contrast, we have grown to be so frozenly proper that we never interrupt a service in any way because, to tell the truth, we are not so particularly glad, we are not so specially full of praise that we want to do anything of the sort. Alas, we have lost very much of the Spirit of God and much of the joy and gladness of His presence, and so we have settled into a decorous apathy! We gather the adornment of propriety instead of the palm branches of praise.

God send us a season of glorious disorder. Oh, for a sweep of wind that will set the seas in motion and make our ironclad brethren now lying so quietly at anchor to roll from stem to stern! Oh, for fire to fall again—fire that shall affect the most reserved! This is a sure remedy for indifference. When a flake of fire falls into a man's bosom, the man knows it, and when the Word of God comes home to a man's soul, the man knows it. Oh, that such fire might first sit upon the disciples and then fall on all around!

To close, there was then *a daily increase* of the church. "And the Lord added to the church daily such as should be saved" (Acts 2:47). Conversion was going on perpetually. Additions to the church were not events that happened once a year but were everyday matters—"So mightily grew the word of God and prevailed" (Acts 19:20).

O Spirit of God, You are ready to work with us today even as You did then! Work, we beseech You, in us. Break down every barrier that hinders the incomings of Your might. Overturn, overturn, O sacred wind! Consume all obstacles, O heavenly fire, and give us now both hearts of flame and tongues of fire to preach Your reconciling word, for Jesus' sake. Amen.

How much there is of church work that is nothing more than the movement of a galvanized corpse! How much is done as if the church were a piece of machinery. While men care little about heart and soul, they look only at outward performances. We can preach, pray, and teach as machines. Men can give mechanically and come to the communion table mechanically. Yes, and we ourselves shall do so unless the Spirit of God is with us. If the Spirit of God is absent, all that the church does will be as lifeless as the rustle of leaves above a tomb, like the congregation of the dead turning over in their graves.

Chapter Two

Our Urgent Need of the Holy Spirit

Through the power of the Holy Ghost . . . by the power of the Spirit of God—Romans 15:13, 19.

WHILE MUCH EMPHASIS has been given to the role of the church as the means through which the multitudes are to be gathered to Jesus Christ, a good deal less attention has been given to the great necessity that exists within the church to accomplish that task—namely, the continual manifestation of the power of the Holy Spirit. Proof of this begins by first showing that the Spirit of God is necessary for the church's own internal growth in grace. From Romans 15:13, "Now the God of hope fill you with all joy and peace in believing, that ye may abound in hope, through the power of the Holy Ghost," it is evident that the apostle attributes to the Holy Spirit the power to fill believers with joy and peace and an abundance of hope.

I want to show also that the power of the church to make an impact upon the world for the gathering in of sinners is this same energy of the Holy Spirit. Reading Romans 15:18–19, the apostle says that God had through him made "the Gentiles obedient, by word and deed, Through mighty signs and wonders, by the power of the Spirit of God."

Two things are clear: to keep the church happy and holy within, there must be a manifestation of the power of the Holy

Spirit, and the church may invade the territories of the enemy and may conquer the world for Christ if she is clothed with the selfsame sacred energy. I contend that the power of the church for external work will be proportionate to the power that dwells within. Gauge the energy of the Holy Spirit in the hearts of believers, and you may fairly calculate the influence of believers upon unbelievers.

Two illustrations help show that external work always depends upon the inward force. On a cold winter's day, you notice that the snow has nearly disappeared from one cottage roof, while another cottage roof still bears a deep coating of snow. The difference is found in a fire burning inside the one cottage and the warmth spreading through the cottage's roof, while the other cottage is without tenant or fire. As the warmth is within, so the melting will be without. I look at a number of churches, and where I see worldliness and formalism lying thick upon them, I am absolutely certain there is not the warmth of Christian life within; but where the hearts of believers are warm with divine love through the Spirit of God, we are sure to see beneficial consequences. We need not look within; in such a case, the exterior is a sufficient index.

Take an illustration from politics. Trouble arises between different nations, and it seems very likely the nations will go to war. One of the hopes of peace lies in the bankrupt condition of the nation that is likely to go to war, for if the nation cannot pay its debts and cannot furnish the material for war, it is unlikely to enter a conflict. A country must be strong in internal resources before it can wisely venture upon foreign wars. The same is true in the great battle of truth: a poor, starving church cannot combat the devil and his armies. Unless the church is herself rich in the things of God and strong with divine energy, she will generally cease to be aggressive and will content herself with going on with the regular routine of Christian work, crying, "Peace! peace!" where peace should not be. She will not dare to defy the world or to send forth her legions to conquer its provinces for Christ when her own condition is pitiably weak. The measure of grace influences the church of God in all her actions.

My point is that you cannot get out of the church what is not in it. The reservoir must be filled before it can pour forth a stream. We must ourselves drink of the living water till we are full, and then out of the midst of us shall flow rivers of living water, but not till then. An empty heart cannot speak life-giving words, and a lean soul cannot produce the abundance that shall feed the people of God. Therefore, the first concern is the church's spiritual health and to pray that God would bless *us* that His way may be known upon earth and His saving power among all people.

The great necessity of the church is to be continuously moved by the power of the Holy Spirit. I write this with the deepest conceivable reverence. Let us adore while we consider this matter. Let us feel the condescension of this blessed Person of the Godhead in choosing to dwell in His people and to work in the human heart. Let us remember that He is a jealous God who is grieved and vexed by the sins of our hearts. With lowliest awe, let us bow before Him, remembering that if there is a sin that is unpardonable, it has a reference to Himself—the sin against the Holy Ghost, which shall never be forgiven. In reference to the Holy Ghost, we stand on very tender ground indeed; and if ever we should veil our faces and rejoice with trembling, it is while we speak of the Spirit and of those mysterious works with which He blesses us. In that lowly spirit, I set before you seven works of the Holy Spirit that are absolutely necessary to the church for her own good and equally needful to her in her office of outreach to the world.

Spiritual Life

To begin, then, the power of the Holy Ghost is manifested in the *quickening* of souls to spiritual life. All the spiritual life that exists in this world is the creation of the Holy Spirit. We did not even realize our spiritual death till He visited us. We had no idea that we were in darkness. We did not have enough sense to feel our misery. We were under sentence of death as condemned criminals, and yet we talked about merit and reward. We were dead and yet boasted that we were alive. The Spirit of God in infinite mercy came to us with His mysterious power and made us live. The first token of life was a consciousness of our being in the realm of death and an agony to escape it. Every growth of spiritual life, from the first tender shoot until now, has been the work of the Holy Spirit. As the green blade was His production, so is the ripening corn. The only way to more life is through the Holy Ghost. You will not even know that you want more unless He works in you to desire it. See, then, our absolute dependence upon the Holy Spirit, for if He were gone, we should relapse in spiritual death, and the church would become a cemetery.

The Holy Spirit is absolutely needful to make everything that we do to be alive. We are sowers, but if we plant dead seed, there will be no harvest. The preacher must preach living truth in a living manner if he expects to obtain a hundredfold harvest. How much there is of church work that is nothing more than the movement of a galvanized corpse! How much is done as if the church were a piece of machinery. While men care little about heart and soul, they look only at outward performances. We can preach, pray, and teach as machines. Men can give mechanically and come to the communion table mechanically. Yes, and we ourselves shall do so unless the Spirit of God is with us. If the Spirit of God is absent, all that the church does will be as lifeless as the rustle of leaves above a tomb, like the congregation of the dead turning over in their graves.

As the Spirit of God is a quickener to make us and our work alive, so must He specially be with us to make those alive with whom we have to deal for Jesus. Imagine a dead preacher preaching a dead sermon to dead sinners. What can possibly come of it? Here is a beautiful essay that has been admirably elaborated, and it is coldly read to the cold-hearted sinner. It smells of midnight oil, but it has no heavenly unction, no divine power resting upon it. It is only as the Spirit of God shall come upon God's servant and shall make the word that he preaches to drop as a living seed into the heart that any result can follow. It is only as the Spirit of God shall then follow that seed and keep it alive in the soul of the listener that we can expect those who profess to be converted to take root and grow to maturity of grace.

We are utterly dependent here, and for my part, I rejoice in this absolute dependence. If I had the power to save souls apart from the Spirit of God, I cannot imagine the temptation to pride and living at a distance from God. It is excellent to be weak in self, and better still to be nothing: to be simply the pen in the hand of the Spirit of God, unable to write a single letter upon the tablets of the human heart except as the hand of the Holy Spirit shall use us for that purpose. That is really our position, and we should continually cry to the Spirit of God to pour His life into all we do and say. We must have a living church for living work. Oh, that God would quicken every member of His church!

Illumination

It is one of the peculiar offices of the Holy Spirit to *enlighten* His people. He has done so by giving us His inspired Word, but the Book is never spiritually understood by anyone apart from the personal teaching of its great Author. You may read it as much as you will and never discover the inner and vital meaning unless your soul is led into it by the Holy Ghost Himself. You may have done well to learn the letter of the truth, but you still need the Spirit of God to make it the light and power of God to your soul. I do not for a moment depreciate a knowledge of the letter, unless you suppose that there is something saving in mere head knowledge. The Spirit of God must come and make the letter alive, transfer it to your heart, set it on fire, and make it burn within you, or else its divine force and majesty will be hid from your eyes. No man knows the things of God save he to whom the Spirit of God has revealed them. No carnal mind can understand spiritual things. You must be taught of the Lord or you will die in ignorance.

When a church has many members who are not taught of the Spirit, evil must and will come of it. Error is sure to arise where truth is not experientially known. Spiritual ignorance will breed conceit, pride, unbelief, and a thousand other evils. With an intense zeal to do good, men have done a world of mischief through a lack of instruction in divine things. Half of the heresy in the church is not willful error but error that springs of not knowing the truth, not searching the Scriptures with a teachable heart, not submitting the mind to the light of the Holy Ghost. If the Spirit of God will but enlighten the church thoroughly, there will be an end of divisions. Schisms are generally occasioned by ignorance and the proud spirit that will not allow correction. On the other hand, real, lasting, practical unity will exist in proportion to the unity of men's minds in the truth of God. Hence the necessity for the Spirit of God to lead us into the whole truth. If you think you know a doctrine, ask the Lord to make you sure that you know it, for much that we think we know turns out to be unknown when times of trial put us to the test. We really know nothing unless it is burnt into our souls as with a hot iron by an experience that only the Spirit of God can give.

The Spirit of God being thus necessary for our instruction, we preeminently find in this gracious operation our strength for the instruction of others, for how shall those teach who have never been taught? How shall men declare a message that they have never learned? "Son of man, eat this roll"; for until you have eaten it yourself, your lips can never tell it to others. "The husbandman that laboureth must first be a partaker of the fruits." It is the law of Christ's vineyard that none shall work there till they first know the flavor of the fruits that grow in the sacred enclosure. You must know Christ and grace and love and truth before you can even be an instructor of babes for Christ.

When we come to deal with others, earnestly longing to instruct them for Jesus, we truly confront our need of the Spirit of God. You think you will articulate the gospel so clearly that they *must* see it, but their blind eyes overcome you. You think you will put it so zealously that they *must* feel it, but their clay-cold hearts defeat you. Old Adam is too strong for young Melancthon. You may think you are going to win souls by your pleadings, but you might as well stand on the top of a mountain and whistle to the wind, unless the Holy Spirit is with you. After all your talking, your hearers will, perhaps, have caught *your* idea, but the mind of the Spirit—the real soul of the gospel—you cannot impart to them. Daily, then, let us pray for the power of the Spirit as the Illuminator. Come, O blessed light of God! You alone can break our personal darkness, and only when You have enlightened us can we lead others in Your light. An ignorant Christian is disqualified for great usefulness; but he who is taught of God will teach transgressors God's ways, and sinners shall be converted to Christ. Both to burn within and shine without you must have the illuminating Spirit.

Adoption

One work of the Spirit of God is to create in believers the spirit of *adoption*. "Because ye are sons, God hath sent forth the Spirit of his Son into your hearts, crying, Abba, Father" (Gal. 4:6). We are regenerated by the Holy Spirit and so receive the nature of children; and that nature, which is given by Him, He continually prompts and excites and develops and matures, so that day by day we receive more and more of the childlike spirit. Now, the church is never happy except as all her members walk as dear children toward God. Sometimes the spirit of slaves creeps over us: we begin to talk of the service of God as though it were heavy and burdensome and are discontented if we do not receive immediate wages and visible success. But the spirit of adoption works for love, without any hope of reward, and it is satisfied with the sweet fact of being in the Father's house and doing the Father's will. This spirit gives peace, rest, joy, boldness, and holy familiarity with God. A man who never received the spirit of a child toward God does not know the bliss of the Christian life; he misses its flower, its savor, its excellence. He does not enjoy the green pastures where the Good Shepherd makes His sheep to feed and to lie down. But when the Spirit of God makes us feel that we are God's children and we live in the house of God, the service of God is sweet and easy, and we accept the delay of apparent success as a part of the trial we are called to bear.

Now mark you, this will have a great effect upon the outside world. A church performing religion as a task, groaning along the ways of godliness with faces full of misery, like slaves who dread the lash, can have but small effect upon the sinners around them. But bring me a church made up of men and women whose faces shine with their heavenly Father's smile, who take their cares and cast them on their Father as children should, who know they are accepted and beloved and are perfectly content with the great Father's will—put them in the midst of sinners, and I guarantee you those sinners will begin to envy them their peace and joy. O blessed Spirit of God! Let us feel that we are the children of the great Father and let our childlike love be warm. So shall we be equipped to proclaim the Lord's love to the prodigals who are in the far-off land among the swine.

Holiness

The Holy Spirit is especially called the Spirit of *holiness*. He has never suggested sin nor approved of it, but holiness is the Spirit's delight. The church of God wears upon her brow the words "Holiness to the Lord." Only in proportion as she is holy may she claim to be the church of God at all. An unholy church! Surely this cannot be she of whom we read, "Christ also loved the church, and gave himself for it; that he might sanctify and cleanse it with the washing of water by the word, that he might present it to himself a glorious church, not having spot, or wrinkle, or any such thing" (Eph. 5:25–27). Holiness is not mere morality, not the outward keeping of divine precepts out of a hard sense of duty while those commandments in themselves are not a delight to us. Holiness is the entirety of our personhood fully consecrated to the Lord and molded to His will. This is the thing that the church of God must have, but it can never have it apart from the Sanctifier, for there is not a grain of holiness beneath the sky but what comes from the Holy Ghost.

If a church is destitute of holiness, what effect can it have upon the world? Scoffers utterly despise those whose inconsistent lives contradict their verbal testimonies. An unholy church may make what noise she can in pretense of working for Christ, but the kingdom does not come to the unholy. The testimony of unholy men is no more acceptable to Christ than was the homage that the evil spirit gave to Him in the days of His flesh, to which He answered, "Hold thy peace." The acts of the church preach more to the world than the words of the church. Put an anointed man to preach the gospel in the midst of a godly people, and his testimony will be marvelously supported by the church; but place the most faithful minister over an ungodly church, and he has such a weight upon him that he must first clear himself of it. He may preach his heart out, he may pray till his knees are weary, but an unholy church makes Christ say that He cannot do many mighty works there because of its iniquity.

Holiness in the church demands the life of the Spirit. When you get to talking to sinners about the necessity of holiness and a renewed heart, do you expect ungodly men to be charmed with what you say? What cares the unregenerate mind for righteousness? As well expect the devil to be in love with God as an unredeemed heart to be in love with holiness. But yet the sinner must love that which is pure and right, or he cannot enter heaven. *You* cannot make him do so. Who can do it but the Holy Ghost who has made you to love what once you also despised? Go not out, therefore, to battle with sin until you have taken weapons out of the armory of the Eternal Spirit. Mountains of sin will not turn to plains at your bidding unless the Holy Ghost is pleased to make the word effectual. So then we see that we need the Holy Spirit as the Spirit of holiness.

Prayer

Fifth, the church needs much *prayer*, and the Holy Spirit is the Spirit of grace and supplication. The strength of a church may be accurately gauged by the church's prayerfulness. We cannot expect God to put forth His power unless we entreat Him to do so. But all acceptable supplication is wrought in the soul by the Holy Ghost. The first desire that God accepts must have been excited in the heart by the secret operations of the Holy One of Israel, and every subsequent pleading of every sort that contains in it a grain of living faith must have been effectually wrought in the soul of Him who makes intercession in the saints according to the will of God. Our great High Priest will put into His censer only the incense that the Spirit has mixed. Prayer is the creation of the Holy Ghost. We cannot do without prayer, and we cannot pray without the Holy Spirit, and hence our dependence on Him.

Furthermore, when we come to deal with sinners, we know that they must pray. "Behold he prayeth" is one of the earliest signs of the new birth. But can *we* make the sinner pray? Can any persuasion of ours lead the sinner to his knees to breathe the penitential sigh and look to Christ for mercy? Let us cry to our heavenly Father to give the Holy Spirit to us. Let us ask Him to be in us more and more mightily as the spirit of prayer, making intercession in us with groanings that cannot be uttered, that the church may not miss the divine blessing for lack of asking for it. I believe this is why the kingdom of Christ does not more mightily spread. Prayer is too much restrained, and the blessing is kept back; and it will always be restrained unless the Holy Ghost shall stimulate the desire of His people. O blessed Spirit, we pray You make us pray, for Jesus' sake.

Fellowship

Sixth, the Spirit of God is in a very remarkable manner the giver of *fellowship*. So often as we pronounce the apostolic benediction, we pray that we may receive the communion of the Holy Ghost. The Holy Ghost enables us to have communion with spiritual things. He alone can take the key and open up the secret mystery that we may know the things of God. He gives us fellowship with God Himself; through Jesus Christ by the Spirit we have access to the Father. Our fellowship is with the Father and His Son Jesus Christ, but it is the Spirit who brings us into communion with the Most High.

So, too, our fellowship with one another is always produced by the Spirit of God. To continue together in peace and love cannot be attributed to our sweet disposition or to wise management or to any natural causes but to the love into which the Spirit has baptized us. If Christian people live together in true spiritual union and unbroken affection, trace it to the love of the Spirit. When believers persevere in service and find themselves loving each other better after many years than they did at the first, let it be regarded as a blessing from the Comforter for which He is to be devoutly adored. Fellowship can come to us only by the Spirit, but a church without fellowship is a kingdom divided against itself. You need fellowship for mutual strength, guidance, help, and encouragement. Without it, your church is a mere human society.

If you are to make an impact upon the world, you must be united as one living body. A divided church has long been the scorn and taunt against Protestants with their divisions. Divisions are our disgrace, our weakness, our hindrance. As the gentle Spirit alone can prevent or heal these divisions by giving us real loving fellowship with God and with one another, how dependent we are upon Him for it. Let us daily cry to Him to work in us brotherly love and all the sweet graces that make us one with Christ, that we all may be one even as the Father is one with the Son, that the world may know that God has indeed sent Jesus and that we are His people.

The Comforter

Seventh, we need the Holy Spirit in that renowned office that is described by our Lord as the *Paraclete*, or Comforter. The word bears another rendering that our translators have given to it in that passage where we read, "If any man sin, we have an *advocate* with the Father" (1 John 2:1). The Holy Spirit is both Comforter and Advocate.

The Holy Spirit is our friend and *Comforter*, sustaining the sinking spirits of believers, applying the precious promises, revealing the love of Jesus Christ to the heart. Many a heart would have broken had not the Spirit of God comforted it. Many of God's children would have utterly died by the way had God not bestowed upon them His divine encouragements. That is His work, and a very necessary work, if believers are to serve with the joy of the Lord as their strength. There are believers whose gloomy lives hinder any evangelism they might hope to do. Till the salt sea yields clusters bursting with new wine, you will never find any unhappy religion promoting the growth of the kingdom of Christ. You must have the joy of the Lord if you are to be strong *in* the Lord and strong *for* the Lord.

We have said that the Spirit of God is the *Advocate* of the church, not with God—for there Christ is our only Advocate—but with man. What is the grandest argument that the church has against the world? I answer, the indwelling of the Holy Ghost, the standing miracle of the church. External evidences are very excellent, but all the evidences of the truth of Christianity that can be gathered are nothing compared with the operations of the Spirit of God.

These are the arguments that convince. A man says to me, "I do not believe in sin, in righteousness, or in judgment." Well, the Holy Ghost can soon convince him. If he asks me for signs and evidences of the truth of the gospel, I point him to believers who once were sinners of the very worst sort. How can the great changes be accounted for? Is it a lie that produces truth, honesty, and love?

What then must that grace be that produces such blessed transformations? The marvelous transforming of moral character is our unanswerable witness. When Peter and John went to the temple and healed the lame man, they were soon brought before the Sanhedrin and asked by what power and by what name they did this. What did they reply? They did not need to say anything, for there stood the man who was healed; the man brought his crutch with him and waved it in triumph, running and leaping. He was their volume of evidences, their apology and proof. "And beholding the man which was healed standing with them, they could say nothing against it" (Acts 4:14).

If we have the Spirit of God among us and lives are being transformed, the Holy Spirit is thus fulfilling His advocacy and refuting all accusers. The Spirit working in your life will always be your best evidence of the gospel. While doubts of every kind will assail your soul over and over again, the power to conquer comes through *personal contact with God*. There is no greater advocate in the soul than the power of the Holy Spirit. We have been stirred to agony under a sense of sin and lifted to ecstasy of delight in faith in the righteousness of Christ. We find that in the little world within our soul the Lord Jesus manifests Himself so that we know Him. There is a potency about the doctrines we have learned that could not belong to lies, for we have tested in actual experience the truths that we believe. Tell us there is no meat? Why, we have just been feasting. Tell us there is no water? We have been quenching our thirst. Tell us there is no spiritual life? We feel it in our inmost souls. These are the answers with which the Spirit of God furnishes us, and they are part of His advocacy.

See, again, how utterly dependent we are on the Spirit of God for meeting all the various forms of unbelief that arise around us. You may write rolls of evidence long enough to circle the globe, but the only person who can savingly convince the world is the Advocate whom the Father has sent in the name of Jesus. When He reveals a man's sin, the unbeliever takes to his knees. When He takes away the scales and sets forth the crucified Redeemer, all carnal reasonings are nailed to the cross. One blow of real conviction of sin will stagger the most obstinate unbeliever; and afterward, if his unbelief returns, the Holy Ghost's consolations will soon comfort it out of him. All this depends upon the Holy Ghost, and upon Him let us wait in the name of Jesus, beseeching Him to manifest His power among us.

Let the Spirit of God reveal to you the pierced hands and feet of Jesus, let Him enable you to put your finger into the prints of the nails and touch the wounds of His feet and lay your heart to His heart—why, if you have no peace, you would be a melancholy miracle of perverse despondency. But you must have rest when you have Jesus Christ, and such a rest that Jesus calls it "My peace," the very peace that is in the heart of Christ, the unruffled serenity of the conquering Savior, who has finished forever the work that God gave Him to do. What rich comfort is this that the Paraclete brings to us!

Chapter Three

The Comforter

And I will pray the Father, and he shall give you another Comforter, that he may abide with you for ever—John 14:16.

THE UNSPEAKABLE GIFT of the Son of God was followed up by the equally priceless gift of the Holy Ghost. Unfortunately, most of us think far less of the Holy Spirit than we should. While we often exalt the Savior and make Him the subject of our thoughts, we give the Holy Spirit a very disproportionate place. I fear that we may even grieve the Spirit by our neglect of Him.

Let me invite you to a serious consideration of the special work of the Holy Spirit. Such an invitation is necessary, for it too seldom occupies our thoughts. Giving too much honor to the Spirit of God is a fault seldom or never committed. We have met people who have glorified the love of Jesus beyond that of the Father, and there are others so occupied with the decrees of the Father as to place the work of the Son into the background; but very few believers have dwelt upon the doctrine of the Holy Spirit beyond its proper measure and degree. The mistake has almost invariably been made in the opposite direction.

The personal name of the Third Person of the Trinity is "the Spirit" or the "Holy Spirit," which describes His nature as being a pure, spiritual, immaterial existence and His character as being in Himself and in His workings preeminently holy. We also commonly speak of Him as the "Holy Ghost," but superstition has degraded the term from its elevated meaning. It might be better if we confined ourselves to the more accurate name, "Holy Spirit," which is His personal title. We have in this verse His official title: He is called the "Comforter," but the word used in the original—*Paraclete*—has a much broader meaning. While "Comforter" is a fair translation, it translates only a corner of the word rather than the whole. It is the light that really streams from the text, but it is one of the seven prismatic colors rather than the combined light of the very instructive and wonderful word *Paraclete*.

How the Holy Spirit Is the *Paraclete*

The *Paraclete* is so profound that it is extremely difficult to convey its full meaning. It is like those Hebrew words that contain so much in a small compass. It is sublime in its simplicity, yet it comprehends great things. Literally, it signifies *called to* or *called beside* another to aid him. It is synonymous verbally, though not in sense, with the the Latin word *advocatus*, a person called in to speak for us by pleading our cause. Yet, as we have come to use the word *advocate* in a different sense, that word also conveys only a part of the meaning.

Paraclete is wider than both. I think the meaning of *Paraclete* might be put under the two headings of *called to* and *calling to*: one called to—that is, to come to our aid, to help our weaknesses, to suggest, to advocate, to guide, and so on; and one who in consequence calls to us. Some see in it the idea of a monitor; and certainly the blessed Paraclete is our teacher, remembrancer, incentive, and comforter. His work as one called in to help us consists very largely in His strengthening us by admonition, by instruction, by encouragement, and by those works that would come under the head of a teacher or a comforter. *Paraclete* is a word too extensive in meaning to be exchanged for any one word in any language. It is most comprehensive, and we shall hope not so much to define as to paraphrase it.

Let us take all the passages in John 14, 15, and 16 that refer to this title and study them with care. From John 14:16 we learn that the Holy Spirit, as the *Paraclete*, is to be to us all that Jesus was to His disciples. "I will pray the Father, and he shall give you *another* Comforter," plainly teaching that the Lord Jesus Christ is the first *Paraclete* and that the Holy Spirit is a second *Paraclete*, occupying the same position as the living Jesus did.

It would be difficult to describe all that Jesus was to His disciples when He dwelt among them. If we call Him their "Guide, Counselor, and Friend," we only begin to list His kindnesses. What a valiant leader is to any army when his very presence inspires them with valor, when his wisdom and strategy conduct them to certain victory, and when his influence over them nerves and strengthens them in the day of battle—all that, and more, was Jesus Christ to His disciples. What the shepherd is to the sheep—the sheep being foolish and the shepherd wise, the sheep being defenseless and the shepherd strong to protect, the sheep being unable to provide for themselves in any degree and the shepherd able to give them all they require—Jesus Christ was to His people.

When you see Jesus, you observe at once that all His disciples are but as little children compared with their Master and that the school would cease immediately if the great Teacher were gone. Jesus is not only the Founder but the Finisher of our system. He is not only the doctor but the doctrine: "I am the way, the truth, and the life" (John 14:6).

The disciples of Christ feel Jesus to be inexpressibly precious. They do not know how many uses Christ can be put to, but this they know—Christ is all in all to them. There is nothing that they have to do or feel or know that is good or excellent, but Jesus Christ enters into it. What would that little company of disciples have been as they went through the streets of Jerusalem without their Lord? Imagine Him absent and no other *Paraclete* to fill His place, and you see no longer a powerful band of teachers equipped to revolutionize the world but a company of fishermen, without skill and without influence, a band that in a short time will melt under the influence of unbelief and cowardice. Christ was all in all to His people while He was here.

All that Jesus was, the Spirit of God is now to the church. He is "another *Paraclete* to abide with us forever." If there is any power in the church of God today, it is because the Holy Spirit is in the midst of the church. If the church is able to work any spiritual miracles, it is through the might of the Spirit's indwelling. If there is any light in her instruction, if there is any life in her ministry, if there is any glory given to God, if there is any good wrought among the sons of men, it is entirely because the Holy Spirit is still with her. The entire weight of influence of the church as a whole—and every Christian in particular—comes from the abiding presence of the sacred *Paraclete*. And we shall do well to treat the Holy Spirit as we would have treated Christ had He been yet among us. Our Lord's disciples told Him their troubles; we must trust the Comforter with ours. Whenever the disciples felt that they were baffled by the adversary, they fell back upon their Leader's power; so must we call in the aid of the Holy Spirit. When the disciples needed guidance, they sought direction from Jesus; we must also seek and abide by the Spirit's leadings. When, knowing what to do but feeling too weak to carry it out, they waited upon their Master for strength; and so must we wait upon the Spirit of all grace. Treat the Holy Spirit with the love and tender respect that are due to the Savior, and the Spirit of God will deal with you as the Son of God did with His disciples.

Moving on in our review of the Scripture passages that relate to the *Paraclete*, we know from John 14:16–17 that the Holy Spirit comforts the people of God by the mere fact of His presence and indwelling. "I will pray the Father, and he shall give you another *Paraclete*, that he may abide with you for ever; . . . for," says the seventeenth verse, "he dwelleth with you, and shall be in you." Is not the mere fact of the presence of the Holy Spirit a comfort to the saints? Jesus has not left you orphans; He has gone, but He has left an equally divine Substitute—the Holy Spirit. If at this moment you do not feel His power, if you are even crying out under a sense of your own natural deadness, yet is it not a comfort to you that there is a Holy Spirit and that the Holy Spirit dwells in you at this present time?

You are not required to bring down the Holy Spirit from heaven. He has come down from heaven and never returned; He dwells in His church perpetually and is not to be brought from on high. He is lawfully to be called upon to work in us, but He is always here. "Oh," you say, "then I have hope, for if the Spirit of God is in me, I know that He will expel my sin. If I were alone and had to fight my spiritual battles alone, I despair; but if it is true that the eternal God Himself, in the majesty of His omnipotence, dwells within my bosom, then, my heart, be of good comfort and be encouraged! The Lord who is in you is mightier than all that are against you." Satan may roar, the lusts of the flesh may assail, but if the Holy Spirit is really resident within the believer's heart, perfection will one day be attained, and the last enemy will be trodden down.

It is consolation to know that the Holy Spirit dwells in us, and He deserves His name of Comforter from the mere fact of His presence and indwelling. But we pass on to notice that according to John 14:26 the Spirit of God exercises His offices as a *Paraclete* and comforts us by His teaching: "The Comforter, which is the Holy Ghost, whom the Father will send in my name, he shall teach you all things, and bring all things to your remembrance, whatsoever I have said unto you." It is part of the Spirit's work to make us *understand* what Jesus taught. If He were merely to bring to remembrance the words of Jesus, it would do us little good; but if you first teach their meaning and then bring the words to remembrance, you have conferred a double and an inestimable blessing. We can, so far as the letter goes, learn from the Scriptures the words of Jesus for ourselves; but to understand these teachings is the gift of the Spirit of God and of no one else. After He takes the key and lets us into the inner meaning of the Lord's words, after He makes us experientially and inwardly to know the force and the power of the truth that Christ revealed, it is very profitable to us to have brought up before our minds the very words of Jesus, and they come to us full of power and sweetness.

What comfort is there in the world equal to the words of Jesus when they are really understood? Is not Jesus Christ Himself "the consolation of Israel"; and, therefore, is not everything that is of Him full of consolation to Israel? If the Spirit of God makes us understand the teachings of Christ, such as His teaching on the pardon of sin by faith and the love of God toward the humble—if those things are actually taught to our souls, the *Paraclete* becomes indeed a Comforter to us. I can teach you the letter of God's Word, but there is One who teaches you to profit effectually and savingly. May He exercise His office upon us.

We note, furthermore, that in this manner, through the Holy Spirit we obtain peace. Observe the verse that follows: "Peace I leave with you, my peace I give unto you: not as the world giveth, give I unto you." He who is taught of God naturally enjoys peace, for if I am taught that my sins were laid on Jesus, how can I help having peace? If I am taught that Jesus intercedes for me before the eternal throne and has taken His blood as my atonement into the holy place, how can I help having peace? And if I am taught the promises of God and made to know that they are "yea and amen in Christ Jesus," how can I be prevented from enjoying peace?

Let the Spirit of God reveal God to you as the everlasting God who loved you before the world was, as the unchanging God who never can turn away His heart from you, and can you do otherwise than rejoice with exceeding great joy? Let the Spirit of God reveal to you the pierced hands and feet of Jesus, let Him enable you to put your finger into the prints of the nails and touch the wounds of His feet and lay your heart to His heart— why, if you have no peace, you would be a melancholy miracle of perverse despondency. But you must have rest when you have Jesus Christ, and such a rest that Jesus calls it "My peace," the very peace that is in the heart of Christ, the unruffled serenity of the conquering Savior, who has finished forever the work that God gave Him to do. What rich comfort is this that the *Paraclete* brings to us!

We have not yet, however, exhausted the meanings, for as we have already said, the word *Paraclete* signifies *advocate*. In his first epistle, John uses this expression: "And if any man sin, we have an advocate with the Father, Jesus Christ the righteous" (1 John 2:1). In the Greek, the passage reads, "If any man sin, we have a *Paraclete* with the Father"—the same word that is here rendered *Comforter*. The word means "advocate" there, and so it must here. The Spirit of God exercises the office of an advocate, but He is not an advocate or intercessor in heaven—our Lord Jesus Christ fills that office.

The Holy Spirit not only intercedes *for* the saints, but He "maketh intercession *for* the saints according to the will of God" (Rom. 8:27). But the Holy Spirit also makes intercession *in* the saints. Let me show this clearly by going back to John 15, where we find the Savior describing His saints in the world as hated and persecuted for His sake. He bids them to expect this, but He consoles them: "But when the Comforter is come, whom I will send unto you from the Father, *even* the Spirit of truth, which proceedeth from the Father, he shall testify of me: and ye also shall bear witness, because ye have been with me from the beginning" (vss. 26, 27). The passage means that while Jesus Christ was here, if anyone had anything to say against Him or His disciples, to the front came the Master, and He soon baffled His foes so that they confessed, "Never man spake like this man."

How are we to answer the attacks of the world today? We have another *Paraclete* to come to the front and speak for us, and if only we had confidence in Him, He would have spoken for us much more loudly than sometimes He has done. But whenever we learn to leave the business in His hands, He will do two things for us: He will speak for us Himself, and He will enable us also to bear witness.

The only way that the church can hold her own and answer her accusers is by real power from God. Has she done anything for the world? Can she produce results? By her fruits shall she be proven to be a tree of life to the nations. The Spirit of God, if we would but trust Him and give up all this idolatry of human learning, cleverness, genius, eloquence, and rhetoric, would soon answer our adversaries. He would silence some of them by converting them, as He answered Saul of Tarsus by turning him from a persecutor to an apostle. He would silence others by confounding them through their own children and relations coming to know the truth.

If there is not a miraculous spiritual power in the church of God today, the church is an impostor. At this moment, the only vindication of our existence is the presence and work of the *Paraclete* among us. Is He still working and witnessing for Christ? Only let men come back to the real gospel and preach it ardently, not with fancy words and polished speech but as a burning heart compels them and as the Spirit of God teaches them to speak it; then will great signs and wonders be seen. We must have signs following; we cannot otherwise answer the world. Let them sneer, let them rave, let them curse, let them lie; God will answer them. It is ours in the power of the Spirit of God to keep on preaching Christ and glorifying the Savior. Just as Jesus always met the adversary in a moment and the disciples had no need of any other defender, so we have another *Paraclete* who in answer to prayer will vindicate His own cause and gloriously avenge His own elect.

We are also promised that this same Spirit will make us witnesses. It shall be given us in the same hour what we shall speak. The Christians who were brought before the Roman tribunals often perplexed their enemies, not by excellency of words and human wisdom but by their holy simplicity and zeal. Christ by His Spirit was manifest in the midst of the early saints, who were victorious through this other *Paraclete* who was with them.

Moreover, the advocacy of the Holy Spirit does not merely relate to the ungodly, but it has to do with ourselves. The Spirit of God is an advocate with us, or within us; He leads us into comfort and advocates our case before the judgment seat of our conscience. This work He does in a manner that is strange to flesh and blood. If the Holy Spirit is an advocate within you, speaking peace within by Jesus Christ, I will tell you how He will plead with you. First, He convinces of sin, showing you to be altogether lost, ruined, and undone, for till self-righteousness is swept away, there will be no consolation. He will convince you of the master sin of having been an unbeliever in Christ, and He will lay you low at the foot of the cross as well as at the foot of Sinai, making you know that you are a sinner against love as well as law, a rebel against the five wounds of Jesus as well as against the ten commands of God: and when He has done this He will convince you of righteousness (John 16:10), that is to say, He will show you that the righteousness of Christ renders you perfectly acceptable with God. He will show you, in fact, that Jesus is "made of God unto thee righteousness." The Spirit of God will comfort you again by bringing home a sense of judgment. He will show you that you and your sins were both judged and condemned on Calvary. He will show you that the evil that now seeks to get the mastery over you was then and there judged and condemned to die, so that you are fighting with a convicted adversary who only lingers for a little while and then shall be entirely dead, even as he now is crucified with Christ.

When the Spirit of God has brought these three things home to you, what an advocate He will be with you! He will say, "Heart, can you now despair? What is there to despair about? Your sin was laid on Jesus. What is there to fear? Oh heart, why lament your lack of righteousness? You have it all in Jesus. Do you fear the coming judgment? You have been judged and condemned in Christ; therefore the sin that is in you shall die, and your inner life shall live eternally."

It is blessed when the Spirit of God argues in our conscience like this. Memory will say, "You did such and such; that will condemn you." But the Spirit of God replies, "I have already condemned this sin, but it was laid upon the great Scapegoat's head and carried away." Then will fear arise and say, "The Lord will visit this man's sin upon him." The Spirit of God will ask, "Who shall lay anything to the charge of God's elect? Is God unrighteous to forget the work and labor of His dear Son?" So with blessed debating power, the Holy Comforter within our soul will plead and intercede in us, and we shall obtain consolation.

Once again, the Holy Spirit is a *Paraclete* according to John 16:13 by His guiding us into all truth, which is, I think, more than was meant by His teaching us all truth. In some parts of the world there are caverns filled with sparkling stalactites. It is helpful to be taught where these caverns are—that is teaching you truth; but it is a better thing when the guide comes forward with his flaming torch and leads you down the winding passages into the great subterranean chambers and holds his flambeau aloft while ten thousand crystals, like stars, vying in color with the rainbow, flash their beams upon you. So not only will the Spirit of God convince you that such and such a teaching is truth, but when He leads you into it so that you experientially know it, taste it, and feel it, then you are admitted to the innermost cave of jewels, where "the diamond lights up the secret mine."

It is a blessed thing when the Spirit of God guides us into all truth. A great many Christians never get *into* the truth. They sit on the outside of it but do not enter in. It is like a great nut to them; they polish the shell and prize it, but if they could once pierce the kernel and taste its flavor, how greatly they would be comforted. John Bunyan used to say he never knew a truth until it was burned into him as with a hot iron. I sympathize deeply with that expression.

There are some truths in the Bible that no one could ever make me doubt because they are interwoven with my vitality. Others are so profitable to my inmost soul that I could not give them up; they are the very life and joy of my being. I know the gospel is true because I have tried and proven its power. I know its inside as well as its outside. I do not merely believe its creed, but its truth is to me real and practical. Hence I say, "Does the fool think he can argue me out of my peace of heart, my joy in the Lord, my hope of heaven?" It cannot be: the mature believer is invulnerable from head to foot against anything and everything that can be hurled against him by skepticism. We are as sure of the truth of the gospel as we are of our own existence. When we hear arguments against our holy faith, all we have to do is just live on in the power of the Spirit and silence gainsayers. May the Holy Spirit thus lead you into all truth—into the secret of the Lord may He conduct you and there feast you on fat things, full of marrow, and upon wines on the lees well refined.

Once more, in John 16:15 we are told that the *Paraclete* glorifies Christ when "he shall take of mine, and shall show it unto you." Could infinite wisdom select a sweeter topic for a troubled heart than "the things of Christ"? When you speak of the things of Christ to a broken heart, you have laid your fingers on the right string. You may bring me the things of Moses and of David, of Solomon and of Daniel, but what are they compared with the things of Christ? Bring me the things of Christ. These are the balm of Gilead, the true medicines of souls diseased. Therefore, the Holy Spirit in His infinite wisdom lifts Jesus up before us, makes Him great in our esteem, glorifies Him in our hearts, and straightway our souls are full of consolation. How could it be otherwise?

The Holy Spirit's Comfort

It is evident from the previous passages that the Spirit of God never dissociates His comfort from character. John 14:15–16 tells us, "If ye love me, keep my commandments. And I will pray the Father, and he shall give you another Comforter." The Spirit of God never comforts a man *in* his sin. Disobedient Christians must not expect consolation; the Holy Spirit sanctifies, and then He consoles. Search and look, see what sin it is that makes you sorrow—obey, and you will be comforted.

The Spirit of God does not purpose to only comfort; He produces peace in the heart as the result of other divinely useful processes. He blesses by purity and then by peace. When a man is feeling pain, he desires that the doctor administer some drug that will immediately stop the unpleasant sensation; yet the doctor refuses, endeavoring to remove the cause of the pain. Isn't the doctor right? So the Spirit of God comforts us by taking away our ignorance and giving us knowledge, by removing our misapprehensions and giving us clear understanding, and by taking away our insensibility and convincing us of sin, of righteousness, and of judgment. Do not expect to get comfort by merely running to sweet texts or listening to pleasing preachers who give you nothing but cups of sugared doctrine. Expect rather to find comfort through the holy, reproving, humbling, strengthening, sanctifying processes that are the operation of the Divine *Paraclete*.

Note next that the comfort of the Holy Spirit is not based upon concealment. While some try to obtain consolation by conveniently forgetting troublesome truth, the Holy Spirit lays the whole truth open before us; He brings all truth to our recollection and hides nothing from us. Therefore, the comfort we obtain from Him is worth having: the consolation, not of fools but of wise men; peace, not for blind bats but for bright-eyed eagles; peace, which age and experience will not invalidate, but which both these will deepen, causing it to grow with our growth and strengthen with our strength. Such is the consolation that the Holy Spirit gives.

Mark and be glad that it is a comfort always in connection with Jesus. If you get near Jesus, you feel you are approaching those comforts that the Spirit intends you to enjoy. Do not run for consolation to mere prophecies of the future or soft reflections about the past. There is a deep well of undefiled consolation by the cross of Christ from which the Eternal Spirit draws full buckets for His thirsty people. Be afraid of the comfort that is not based upon truth. Hate the comfort that does not come from Christ. Water from the well of Bethlehem is what you want.

It is comfort, too, that is always available. The comforts of the Holy Spirit do not depend upon health, strength, wealth, position, or friendship; the Holy Spirit comforts us through the truth, and the truth does not change. The Holy Spirit comforts us through Jesus, and He is "yea and amen"; therefore, our comforts may be as real when we are dying as when we are in health, and our consolations may be even more abounding when the purse is empty than when all the world's wealth and pleasure abound to us. This is the comfort of the Spirit that brought the martyrs to stand before their accusers and to face death with unblanching cheek; it was the comfort of the Holy Spirit that led the Waldensians to count not their lives dear to them; it made Luther so brave in the face of death. Many a believer died in ecstasy under the power of this consolation. If you know the Holy Ghost as your *Paraclete*, you will never require another consolation.

Conclusions

Honor the Spirit of God as you would honor Jesus Christ if He were present. If Jesus Christ were dwelling in your house, you would not ignore Him, you would not go about your business as if He were not there. Do not ignore the presence of the Holy Ghost in your soul. Give constant adoration to Him. Reverence the august Guest who has been pleased to make your body His sacred abode. Love Him, obey Him, worship Him.

Take care to never impute the vain imaginings of your fancy to Him. I have seen the Spirit of God shamefully dishonored by persons who said that they have had this and that revealed to them. For the past several years, not a single week has passed in which I have not been pestered with the revelations of hypocrites and very strange sorts of people. These people are very fond of coming with messages from the Lord to me, and it may spare them some trouble if I tell them once for all that I have nothing to do with their stupid messages. When my Lord and

Master has any message to me, He knows where I am, and He will send it to me direct. Never dream that events are revealed to you by heaven, or you may come to be like those idiots who dare impute their blatant follies to the Holy Ghost. If you feel your tongue itch to talk nonsense, trace it to the devil, not to the Spirit of God. Whatever is to be revealed by the Spirit to any of us is in the Word of God already—the Spirit of God adds nothing to the Bible, and never will. Let persons who have revelations of this, that, and the other *go to bed and wake up in their senses.* I only wish they would no longer insult the Holy Ghost by laying their nonsense at His door.

At the same time, since the Holy Spirit is with you, in all your learning, ask Him to teach you; in all your suffering, ask Him to sustain you; in all your teaching, ask Him to give you the right words; in all your witnessing, ask Him to give you constant wisdom; and in all service, depend upon Him for His help. Believingly depend upon the Holy Spirit. We seldom take Him in our calculations as we should. We add up so many missionaries, so much money, and so many schools, and so conclude the list of our forces. The Holy Spirit is our great need, not learning or culture. Little knowledge, or great knowledge, shall answer almost as well if the Spirit of God is there; but all your knowledge shall be worthless without Him. Let the Spirit of God come, and what a difference He brings. You have a Sunday school class that you feel unable to teach; ask Him to help you, and you may be surprised how well you will teach. You are asked to preach but feel you cannot; bring the Holy Spirit into it, and if He fires you, you shall find even the slender materials you have collected will set the people ablaze. We should count upon the Spirit; He is our main and only force, and we grieve Him exceedingly when we do not depend upon Him. Love the Spirit, worship the Spirit, trust the Spirit, obey the Spirit, and as a church, cry mightily to the Spirit. Beseech Him to let His mighty power be known and felt among you. The Lord fire your hearts with the sacred flame that made Pentecost stand out from all other days. Come, Holy Spirit now! You are with us, but come with power and let us feel Your sacred might.

Lift up your eyes to the hills and mark how the breeze courses along the downs and sweeps the summits of the mountain ranges. In the morning and the evening, when the inland air is hot as an oven, gentle winds come to and from the sea and fan the fisherman's cheek. You may find places where the air seems always stagnant and men's hearts grow heavy amid the feverish calm, but there are elevated hillsides where life is easy, for the air exhilarates by its perpetual freshness. Mark this well: among God's saints, in the use of the means of grace, in private prayer, in communion with the Lord, you will find the wind that blows where it wills always in motion.

Chapter Four

The Heavenly Wind

The wind bloweth where it listeth, and thou hearest the sound thereof, but canst not tell whence it cometh, and whither it goeth: so is every one that is born of the Spirit—John 3:8.

THE HOLY SPIRIT is to be admired not only for the great truths that He teaches us in Holy Scripture but also for the wonderful manner in which those truths are balanced. The Word of God never gives us too much of one thing or too little of another: it never carries a doctrine to an extreme, but tempers it with its corresponding doctrine. Truth seems to run at least in two parallel lines, if not three; and when the Holy Spirit sets one before us, He wisely points out the other as well. The truth of divine sovereignty is qualified by human responsibility, and the teaching of abounding grace is seasoned by a remembrance of unflinching justice. Scripture gives, as it were, the acid and the base; the rock and the oil that flows from it; the cutting sword and the balm that heals. The Holy Spirit sends out His truths two by two that each may help the other for the blessing of those who hear.

In this most notable third chapter of John there are two truths taught as plainly as if they were written with a sunbeam, and taught side by side. The one is the necessity of faith in the Lord Jesus and the fact that whoever believes in Him is not condemned. This is a vital doctrine, but there is a possibility of preaching it so exclusively that men may be led into serious error. Justification by faith is a most precious truth—it is the very heart of the gospel—and yet you can so dwell upon it that you cause many to forget other important practical truths, and so do them serious harm. Salt is good, but it is not all that a man needs to live upon, and even if people are fed the best of bread and nothing else, they do not thrive. Every part of divine teaching is of practical value and must not be neglected. Hence, the Holy Ghost in this chapter lays equal stress upon the necessity of the new birth or the work of the Holy Spirit, and He states it just as plainly as the other grand truth. See how they blend—"Ye must be born again" (John 3:7); but "whosoever believeth in him should not perish, but have eternal life" (John 3:15); "Except a man be born of water and of the Spirit, he cannot enter into the kingdom of God" (John 3:5); but "He that believeth on him is not condemned" (John 3:18).

Two great truths are written in letters of light over the gate of heaven as prerequisites of all who enter there—*Reconciliation by the blood of Jesus Christ* and *Regeneration by the work of the Holy Ghost*. We must not put one truth before the other or allow one to obliterate or hide the other: they are of equal importance, for they are revealed by the same Spirit and are alike needful to eternal salvation. He who cares to preach either of these ought also diligently teach the other. Avoid all neglect of faith and equally shun all undervaluing of the work of the Holy Spirit. So shall you find that narrow channel in which the way of truth lies. You must rest in Christ that you are accepted by God, but the work of the Holy Spirit within you is absolutely needful that you may be able to have communion with the pure and holy God. Faith gives us the rights of the children of God, but the new birth must be experienced that we may have the nature of children: of what use would rights be if we did not have the capacity to exercise them?

It is of the work of the Spirit of God—and of the man in whom the Spirit of God has worked—that Jesus refers to in the text. John 3:8 may be read two ways. First, it clearly refers to *the Holy Spirit Himself*. Do you not expect the text to read: "The wind bloweth where it listeth, and thou hearest the sound thereof, but canst not tell whence it cometh, and whither it goeth; so also is the Spirit of God"? Isn't that the way you naturally expect the sentence to end? Yes, and I do not doubt that was the Savior's meaning; but frequently, according to the New Testament idiom, the truth is not stated as our English modes of speech would lead us to expect. For instance, "The kingdom of heaven is like unto a man that sowed good seed in his ground." The kingdom is not like the man but like the whole transaction of the parable in which the man is the principal actor. So here in John 3:8, the Lord Jesus lays hold of one grand sphere of the Spirit's operations and puts it down, intending, however, a wider sense.

There are certain translations of our text that make this clearer, for instance, that which does not render the Greek word by "wind" at all but translates it "spirit"—"The Spirit bloweth where He listeth . . ." I do not adopt that reading, but there are several great authorities that do, and this tends to show that our first point is correct. Once I have developed this idea, I will move on to its second sense, in reference to *the regenerate man*. Then we read, "The wind bloweth where it listeth, and thou hearest the sound thereof, but canst not tell whence it cometh, and whither it goeth; so is every man that is born of the Spirit." The regenerate man, like the Spirit of which he is born, is free and is mysterious in his ways but discerned by the sound of his works and life.

The Holy Spirit Himself

The figure utilized is the wind. It should be pointed out that the Hebrew word for "wind" and for "spirit" is the same; and it is interesting to note that the same is true with the Greek word *pneuma*, which is translated both "breath" and "spirit." The wind is air in motion and is material; but air is apparently more spiritual than any of the other elements, except fire, since it cannot be grasped by the hand or seen with the eye. It is certain that wind truly exists, for we hear its sound and observe its various effects although it cannot be touched, handled, or gazed upon. We may watch the clouds hastened along like the birds, but the wind that drives them is beyond our sight. We observe the waves roused to fury in the tempest, but the breath that so excites them we cannot see. Hence the word becomes all the more excellent a figure of that mighty power—the Holy Ghost—of whose existence no person ever doubts who has come under His influence, but who nevertheless is not to be traced in His movements or seen as to His divine person, for He is mysterious, incomprehensible, and divine.

The metaphor of the wind cannot fully set forth the Holy Spirit. Consequently, many other natural figures are employed, such as fire, dew, water, light, and oil, in order to exhibit more of the phases of His influence. But still the wind is a most instructive metaphor as far as it goes, and from it we draw the following lessons.

The Holy Spirit's Freeness

First, the wind speaks of the Holy Spirit's *freeness*—"The wind bloweth where it listeth." We speak of the wind as the very image of freedom: we claim to be "free as the winds which roam at their own will." No one can fetter the wind. Xerxes threw chains into the Hellespont to bind the sea, but even he was not fool enough to talk of forging fetters for the winds. The breezes are not to be dictated to. Caesar may decree what he pleases, but the wind will blow in his face if he looks that way. No proclamation or purpose under heaven will be able to affect the wind by so much as half a point of the compass. The wind will blow according to its own sweet will, where it pleases, when it pleases, how it pleases, and as it pleases, for "the wind bloweth where it listeth."

So it is—only in a far higher and more emphatic sense—with the Holy Spirit, for He is most free and absolute. The Holy Spirit is God Himself, and absolutely free, and works according to His own will and pleasure among the sons of men. One nation has been visited by the Holy Spirit and not another—who shall tell me why? Why the dense darkness over some nations, while on others the light has been concentrated? Why did the Reformation take root in England and northern Europe, while in Spain and Italy it hardly left a trace? Is it not that He does as He wills? "I will have mercy on whom I will have mercy, and I will have compassion on whom I have compassion" is the declaration of the divine sovereignty, and the Spirit of God in His movements confirms it. How is it that two people hearing the same sermon and subject to the same influences respond so differently to its message? Two children loved and trained in the same household grow up to different ends. He who perishes in sin has no one to blame but himself, but he who is saved ascribes it all to grace—why did that grace come to him? We dare not lay the fault of man's not repenting and believing upon God—that rests with the evil will that refused to obey the gospel. We dare not ascribe the saving difference in the case of the one who believes to any natural goodness in himself, but we attribute it all to the grace of God and believe that the Holy Spirit works in such to will and to do according to His own good pleasure. But why did He work in us? Why in anyone? Ah, why? "The wind bloweth where it listeth."

So, too, is this shown with the blessing that rests upon ministries. One person wins souls to Christ and as a joyous reaper returns with full sheaves, but another goes forth with intense zeal and comes home with a scanty handful of ears that he has painfully gleaned. Why is one man's net full and another's utterly empty? One servant of the Lord seems, whenever he stands up to preach, to attract men to Jesus as though he had golden chains in his mouth that he cast about men's hearts to draw them in joyful captivity to his Lord, while another cries in despair, "Who hath believed our report?" Truly, "the wind bloweth where it listeth."

Note also the changes within a person: one day the preacher's spirit is stirred within, and he speaks powerfully with the Holy Ghost sent down from heaven; but tomorrow he finds himself dull and heavy, even to his own consciousness, and even more so to his people's experience, for the power does not rest upon him. One day he speaks like the voice of God, and another day he is a reed shaken by the wind. Today he comes forth with the unction of the Lord upon him and his face shining with the glory of fellowship with the Most High, and tomorrow he says, "Look not upon me, for the glory has departed." Any preacher knows what it is to come forth like Samson when his locks had been cut and discover the Lord is not with him. Why all this? Is it not because "the wind bloweth where it listeth"? The Holy Spirit, for His own wise reasons, does not put forth an equal power upon any person at all times. We cannot control or command the Spirit of the living God: He is in the highest sense a free agent. "Thy free Spirit" is a name that David gave Him, and a most appropriate name it is.

Yet we should not fall into a misapprehension. The Holy Ghost is absolutely free in His operations, but He is not arbitrary; He does as He wills, but His will is infallible wisdom. The wind, though we have no control over it, has a law of its own, and the Holy Spirit is a law unto Himself; He does as He wills, but He wills to always do what is for the best. Moreover, we know with regard to the wind that there are certain places where you will almost always find a breeze: not here in the crowded city, or down in the valley shut in by the mountains, or on yonder steaming marsh; but lift up your eyes to the hills and mark how the breeze courses along the downs and sweeps the summits of the mountain ranges. In the morning and the evening, when the inland air is hot as an oven, gentle winds come to and from the sea and fan the fisherman's cheek. You may find places where the air seems always stagnant and men's hearts grow heavy amid the feverish calm, but there are elevated hillsides where life is easy, for the air exhilarates by its perpetual freshness. Mark this well: among God's saints, in the use of the means of grace, in private prayer, in communion with the Lord, you will find the wind that blows where it wills always in motion.

The wind, too, has times and seasons. We know that at certain times of the year we may expect winds, and if the winds do not come to a specific day, yet as a rule, the month is stormy. And there are trade winds, monsoons that blow with remarkable regularity and are counted upon by mariners. And so with the Spirit of God. We know that at certain times He visits the churches and under certain conditions puts forth His power. If, for instance, there is mighty prayer, you may be sure the Spirit of God is at work. If the people of God meet together and besiege the throne of grace with cries and tears, the spiritual barometer indicates that the blessed wind is rising. Besides, the Holy Spirit has graciously connected Himself with two things: truth and prayer. Preach the truth, publish the gospel of Jesus Christ, and it is the habit of the Holy Spirit to make the word quick and powerful to the hearts of men. If we falsify His word, if we keep back part of the truth, if we become unfaithful, we cannot expect the Holy Spirit to bless us; but if our teaching is Christ crucified, lovingly set forth, and if the grace of God in its fullness is really declared, the Holy Spirit will accompany the truth and make it the great power of God.

I will not say that is always the case, but I think exceptions must be rare. Almost invariably the Spirit bears witness with the truth in the conversion of men. So too with prayer. The Holy Spirit is pleased to connect Himself with that also, if it is believing prayer. Here the connection is exceedingly intimate because it is the Spirit of God who Himself gives birth to believing prayer; and not only is it true that the Spirit will be given in answer to prayer, but the Spirit is already given or the believing prayer would never have been offered. The spirit of prayerfulness, the spirit of anxiety for the conversion of men is one of the surest indications that the Holy Spirit is already at work in the minds of His people.

What influence should the great fact that we cannot command the Holy Spirit have upon us? It should lead us to be very tender and jealous in our conduct toward the Holy Ghost so that we do not grieve Him and cause Him to depart from us. "Vex not the Spirit." When you enjoy His gracious operations, be devoutly grateful and walk humbly before God, that you may retain them; and when He is at work, let not negligence on your part cause you to receive the grace of God in vain. The wind blew, but the sailor slept; it was a favorable breeze, but he had cast anchor. If he had known it, all through the night he would have spread his sail and made good headway toward his port; but he slumbered, and the blessed wind whistled through the cordage, and the ship lay idle at its moorings. Let it not be so with us. Never allow the Spirit of God to be with us and find us inattentive to His presence.

In ancient times, country people depended on the use of the windmill to grind their corn, and they suffered dearly when week after week there was no wind. The miller would look up anxiously, and everyone would become a watchman for his sails, hoping that the sails would soon be set in motion. If the breeze stirred in the dead of night, someone would run and wake the miller. "The wind is blowing, the wind is blowing, grind our corn." So it should be whenever the Spirit of God is vigorously working in His church—we should eagerly avail ourselves of His power. We should be so anxious for His divine operations that all should be on the watch so that if some did not discover it, others would; and observant ones would cry, "The Holy Spirit is working with us; let us arise and labor more abundantly." Hoist sail when the wind blows; you cannot command it, therefore carefully value it.

The Holy Spirit's Manifestations

The Holy Spirit is described as being like the wind as to *His manifestations*. "Thou hearest," says Jesus, "the sound thereof." There are many manifestations of the presence of wind: you can feel it, you can see its results, and sometimes you can be sure that the wind has been at work by the devastation that it has caused. But in this place, our Savior was not so much alluding to the great wind as to the gentler breezes. The Greek work *pneuma* is translated "breath" and can hardly be made to mean a tempest. It is a gentle breeze of which the Lord is speaking. The great winds can be somewhat calculated upon, but if you sit in the garden in the cool of the evening, it is utterly impossible to tell how the breezes come and where they go. They are so volatile in their movements and untrackable in their course. Here, there, everywhere, the soft breezes of evening steal among the flowers.

Our Lord tells us that such gentle zephyrs are heard: Nicodemus could hear them in the stillness of the night. The leaves rustle, and that is all. A gentle movement of branch and stem and, as it were, the tinkling of flower-bells, and so you discover that the wind is flitting among the beds and borders. This shows that the hearing ear is intended by God to be the discerner of the Spirit to men and, to most men, the only discerner that they have. "Thou hearest the sound thereof." What a wonderful dignity the Lord has been pleased to give this little organ, the ear.

The church has often given preference to the eye, astonishing people with wonderful priestly performances; but God's way is "faith cometh by hearing" (Rom. 10:17), and the first detector of the Holy Ghost is the ear. To most, this is the only revealer of His mysterious presence: they hear the sound, that is to say, they hear the gospel preached, they hear the Word of God read. Truth when it is couched in words is the rustling of the holy wind, it is the footstep of the Eternal Spirit as mysteriously He passes along the congregation. Oh what grief it is that some never get any further than this but abide where Nicodemus was at that moment: they hear the sound and nothing more. When you hear the rustling among the boughs of the trees, the breezes are not far to seek, nor is the Spirit of God far away when His sound is heard.

Some hearers, however, go further, for they hear the sound of the Spirit in their consciences, and it disturbs them. The wind sometimes comes whistling through the keyhole or howls down the chimney and wakes them. So is it with many unconverted people; they cannot be quiet, for they hear the sound of the Holy Spirit in their consciences and are troubled and perplexed. There is a revival, and they are not saved, but they are startled and alarmed by it. Their sister is converted, they are not, but still it comes near them, and they feel as if an arrow had gone whizzing by their ear. It is hard living in a careless state in the midst of revival. Something mighty is at work, but they do not experience its regenerating power.

The person who is a Christian hears the Holy Spirit in the most emphatic sense, and with an amazing variety, that sound comes to him. At first he heard it as a threatening wind, which bowed him in sadness and seemed to sweep all his hopes to the ground, as the leaves of the forest are carried in the autumn's wind. When the Spirit's voice first sounded in my ears, it was as a wail of woe, as a wind among the tombs, as a sigh among faded lilies. It seemed as if all my hopes were blown away like smoke; nothing was left for me but to mourn my nothingness. Then I heard a sound as of the hot sirocco of the East, as if it issued from a burning oven. "The grass withereth, the flower fadeth: because the spirit of the Lord bloweth upon it: surely the people is grass" (Isa. 40:7). In my soul there had bloomed a fair meadow of golden kingcups and fair flowers of many dainty colors, but the Spirit of God blew on them and withered it all, leaving only a dry, brown, rusty plain of lifelessness.

So far the sacred wind destroys that which is evil, but it does not end there, for we thank God we have heard the sound of the Spirit as a quickening wind. The prophet cried, "Come from the four winds, O breath, and breathe upon these slain, that they may live" (Ezek. 37:9); the wind came and the dead arose. A similar miracle has been worked in us. The old bones of our own death have crept together, bone unto His bone; and flesh has come upon them, and now because of the divine breath, we have begun to live. Now, also, when the Holy Spirit visits us, He renews our life and energy, and we have life more abundantly.

The Holy Spirit has since often been like a melting wind: "He causeth His wind to blow and the waters flow." Locked up in the chains of ice all through the winter, the waters are still as a stone; but the spring winds come, and the tiny brooks find liberty and leap away to the rivers; and the rivers flow in all their free force to add their volume to the sea. So has the Spirit of God oftentimes broken up our frost and given our spirits joyous liberty. He melts the rocky heart and dissolves the iron spirit; at the sound of His presence, men are moved to feeling. We know the sound of this wind also as a diffusive breath, drawing forth and diffusing our slumbering graces. "Awake, O north wind; and come, thou south; blow upon my garden, that the spices thereof may flow out" (Sol. 4:16).

Oh what a sweet unloosing of holy gratitude and love and hope and joy has there been in our hearts when the Spirit of God has visited us. As sweet perfumes lie hidden in the flowers until the loving wind entices them to fly abroad, so do sweet graces lie within renewed spirits until the Holy Ghost comes and speaks to them, and they know His voice and come forth to meet Him, and so sweet fragrances are shed abroad.

We have heard the sound of the Holy Spirit in another sense—namely, as going forth with us to the battle of the Lord. We have heard that sound of a breeze in the tops of the mulberrry trees that David heard, and we have bestirred ourselves, and the victory has been ours. If we have not heard that rushing mighty wind that came at Pentecost, yet have we felt its divine effect, which never ceases but always brings life, power, energy, and all that is needed for those of us called to go forth and preach the gospel among the nations. In all these respects, the Holy Ghost has manifested Himself as wind does, by His sound.

The Holy Spirit's Mystery

A third likeness of the Spirit to the wind is *mystery*. "Thou canst not tell whence it cometh nor whither it goeth." We may tell a certain direction that the wind comes from, but no one can point to a map and say, "The north wind began here." Indeed, we know very little about the winds, their origin, or their laws. We do not know where the winds first spread their wings or where they sleep when all is still. So it is with the Holy Spirit in the mind of man; His first movements are hidden in mystery. You know that you are converted and probably remember somewhat as to the means that the Lord used for your salvation. Those outward circumstances you know, but you cannot explain how the Holy Spirit worked in you anymore than you can explain how the life swells within the seed until it springs up and becomes the full corn in the ear. There are secrets that nature does not reveal, and the work of the Spirit is even more a secret, and assuredly no man can explain it to his fellow or to himself. Why is it that you obtained a blessing through one sermon but not from another, and yet when you spoke to someone else, he had been more blessed under the second than the first? It is clear, then, that the power does not come from the preacher, and "thou canst not tell whence it comes."

There are times in which you feel not only that you can pray but also that you must pray. Why is that? I know what it is to feel a very ecstasy of delight in the Lord for which I cannot explain and yet find at other times no consciousness of any such exceeding delight in God. At one time the heart will be full of brokenness over sin, and at another season it will overflow with such delight in Christ that the sin seems almost forgotten. Why these diverse workings? And explain how these various workings of the Spirit come? Go trace the dewdrops, if you can, to the womb of the morning, and discover which way the lightning's flash went and how the thunder rolled along the mountaintops, but you cannot tell, nor can you guess, how the Spirit of God comes into your soul.

Nor can we tell where it goes. Here, again, is another mystery. It charms me to think that when we declare the truth in the power of the Spirit we never know where it will fly. A child takes a seed, one of those little downy seeds that has its own parachute to carry it through the air. The little one blows it into the air, but who knows where that downy seed shall settle or in whose garden it shall grow? Such is truth, even from the mouths of babes. Scatter the truth on all sides, for you cannot tell where the Spirit will carry it. Fling it to the winds, and you will find it after many days. Scatter the living seed with both hands, send it north, south, east, and west, and God will give it wings.

> Waft, waft ye winds the story,
> And you, ye waters roll,
> Till like a sea of glory
> It spreads from pole to pole.

I recently received a letter from a sister in Christ in Brazil. She said she had read a copy of my *Morning Readings* and through its message found the way of peace. She wrote me such a loving, touching letter that it brought tears to my eyes. At the end was another's handwriting, some word to the effect that his dear wife who had written the letter had died soon after finishing it; and with a bleeding heart, the lone husband sent it on to me rejoicing that the word came to his wife's soul in a far-off land. You do not know where the word will go and the Spirit with it. A truth will go down through the centuries—like the river, it sings:

> Men may come and men may go,
> But I go on forever.

"Thou canst not tell whither it goeth." It will travel on till the millennium. Send that saying abroad that the truth cannot die. The persecutor cannot kill it; it is immortal, like the God who sent it forth. The persecutor cannot even stay its course; it is divine. So long as there is one page of the Bible upon earth or one person living who knows the Savior, the Antichrist cannot triumph. The Holy Spirit wars against it with the sword of the Word, and you cannot tell how far into the heart of error any truth may be driven. To the overthrow of falsehood and the death of sin, the Spirit speeds on; but you never know how.

"Thou canst not tell whither it goeth" either in anyone's heart. If you have received the Holy Spirit, you cannot tell where He will lead you. I am sure that William Carey, when he gave his young heart to Christ, never thought the Spirit of God would carry him to Serampore to preach the gospel to the Hindus. And when George Whitefield first drank of the lifegiving Spirit, it never occurred to him that the potboy at the Bell Inn at Gloucester would thunder the gospel over two continents and turn thousands to Christ. No! You do not know to what blessed end this wind will blow you. Commit yourselves to it: be not disobedient to the heavenly vision; be ready to be borne along as the Spirit of God shall help you, even as the dust in the summer's breeze. And child of God, you do not know to what heights of holiness and degrees of knowledge and ecstasies of enjoyment the Spirit of God will bear you. "Eye hath not seen, nor ear heard, . . . the things which God hath prepared for them that love him" (1 Cor. 2:9); and though He has revealed them by His Spirit, yet even the best taught child of God does not yet know the full wonders of the Spirit of God. "Trust ye in the LORD forever, for in the LORD JEHOVAH is everlasting strength" (Isa. 26:4); and He will bear you onward and upward, even to perfection itself; and you shall be with Jesus, where He is, and behold His glory.

Those Who Are Born of the Spirit

"The wind bloweth where it listeth, and thou hearest the sound thereof, but canst not tell whence it cometh, and whither it goeth: so is every one that is born of the Spirit." The child partakes of the nature of the parent. That which is born of the Spirit is like unto the Spirit of which it is born. The twice-born man is like the Holy Ghost who produced him, and he is like Him in each of the points that we have already dwelt upon in this chapter. As to *freedom*, you may say of him, "He bloweth where he listeth." The Spirit of God makes the believer a free man, bestows on him the freedom of His will that he never had before, and gives him a delightful consciousness of liberty. "If the Son therefore shall make you free, ye shall be free indeed" (John 8:36).

I do not affirm that every spiritual man does as the Spirit wills, because, alas, I see another law in our members warring against the law of our mind and bringing us into captivity to the law of sin and death: but still, "where the Spirit of the Lord is, there is liberty" (2 Cor. 3:17). Now you can pray like you could not before; now you can praise though you could not extract a note of praise from your ungrateful heart before; now you can cry, "Abba, Father"; now you can draw near to God. You are no longer under man's control, you blow where you will; you are not controlled by the opinion of others. The Lord has set you free to go where His word bids you go, and you find the utmost liberty in going that way.

I cannot describe the change felt by a regenerate man in the matter of spiritual liberty. When you were under the bondage of the law, of religious customs and of sin, and of fear of death and dread of hell, you were like a man shut up in one of those cells in Venice that lie below sea level, where the air is foul and the prisoner can stir only a half a dozen feet and then walk back again in the darkness. But when the Spirit of God comes, He brings the soul from darkness into light, from clammy damp into the open air. He sets before you an open door. He helps you to run in the ways of God's commands. And as if that were not enough, He even lends you wings and bids you mount as the eagle, for He has set you free.

The man who is born of the Spirit will be *manifested* by his sound. "Thou hearest the sound thereof." The secret life within will speak. Words there will be, for Christians are not silent. But actions will speak more loudly still; and even apart from actions, the very spirit and tone of the person who is really regenerated will speak, and the ungodly will be compelled to hear.

And now notice *the mystery* there is about a Christian. The unspiritual person knows nothing about the life the believer leads, for he is dead and his life is hid with Christ in God. He cannot understand the strength with which the believer comes forth in the morning, those beds of spices that have made his garments fragrant, that weeping in prayer or that rejoicing in fellowship with which he opened the morning. Neither can the unbeliever tell where the spiritual man goes. In the midst of his trouble, the unbeliever sees the believer calm. Where does the spiritual man secure that rare quietude? In the hour of death explain the triumph? There is a secret place of the Most High, and they shall abide under the shadow of the Almighty who have once learned to enter there, but carnal men come not into this secret chamber.

The Christian life is a mystery from beginning to end: to the worldling all a mystery and to the Christian a puzzle. The Christian cannot read his own riddle or understand himself. This one thing he knows: "Whereas I was blind, now I see" (John 9:25). This also "O Lord, truly I am thy servant; I am thy servant, and the son of thine handmaid: thou hast loosed my bonds" (Ps. 116:16). And he knows that when his Lord shall be revealed, then will he also shine forth like the sun. The life within him is a mystery to him, but he blesses God that he has fellowship in it. He goes on his way feeling that though men do not understand his life nor does he know where he is going, yet the Lord knows him, and he is sure that he is ultimately going to his Father and his God. Oh, that every reader had so delightul a hope! The Lord grant it to you for Jesus' sake.

Oh, to see the love of Christ in the light of the Holy Ghost! When it is truly revealed to us, we wonder if we ever understood anything before. The Holy Ghost shows us the naked truth, the essence of the love of Christ; and what that essence is— that love without beginning, without change, without limit, without end; and that love set upon His people simply from motives within Himself—what that must be, what tongue can tell? It is a ravishing sight!

Chapter Five

"Honey in the Mouth!"

He shall glorify me: for he shall receive of mine, and shall show it unto you. All things that the Father hath are mine: therefore said I, that he shall take of mine, and shall show it unto you—
John 16:14–15.

JESUS SPEAKS HERE of the Trinity, and especially of the role of the Holy Spirit in our lives. It is wise to always keep the Trinity prominent before you. Remember, you cannot even truly pray without the Trinity. If the full work of salvation requires a Trinity, so does the very breath by which we live. You cannot draw near to the Father except through the Son and by the Holy Spirit. There is a trinity in nature undoubtedly. There certainly constantly turns up the need of a Trinity in the realm of grace. When we get to heaven, we shall understand, perhaps, more fully what is meant by the Trinity in unity. But if that is a thing never to be understood, we shall at least comprehend it more lovingly, and we shall rejoice more completely as the three tones of our music shall rise up in perfect harmony to Him who is one and indivisible and yet is three, forever blessed, Father, Son, and Holy Ghost, one God.

It should never be understated: there is no salvation apart from the Trinity. It must be the Father, the Son, and the Holy Ghost. "All things that the Father hath are mine," says Christ;

and the Father has all things. They were always His; they are still His; they always will be His; and they cannot become ours till they change ownership, till Christ can say, "All things that the Father hath are mine," for it is by virtue of the representative character of Christ standing as the assurance of the covenant that the "all things" of the Father are passed over to the Son, that they might be passed over to us. "It pleased the Father that in him should all fulness dwell" (Col. 1:19); "and of his fulness have all we received" (John 1:16). And yet we are so spiritually dull that though the conduit pipe is laid to the great fountain, we cannot get at it. We are too lame to reach it; and in comes the third Person of the divine unity—even the Holy Spirit—and He receives of the things of Christ and then delivers them to us. So we do actually receive what is in the Father.

Ralph Erskine prefaced a sermon upon this fifteenth verse with this unforgettable analogy. He speaks of grace as honey— honey for the cheering of the saints, for the sweetening of their mouths and hearts. But he says that in the Father "the honey is in the flower, which is so far from us that we could never extract it." In the Son "the honey is in the comb, prepared for us in our Immanuel, God-Man Redeemer, the Word that was made flesh, saying, 'All things that the Father hath are mine'; it is in the comb. But then, next, we have honey in the mouth; the Spirit taking all things and making application by showing them to us and making us to eat and drink with Christ and share of these 'all things'; yes, not only eat the honey, but also the honeycomb; not only His benefits, but Himself."

What a wonderful picture! Honey in the flower in God—as in mystery—really there. There never will be any more honey than there is in the flower. There it is. But how shall you and I get at it? We do not have the wisdom to extract the sweetness. We are not equipped as the bees are. It is bee honey, but not man honey. Yet you see in Christ that it becomes the honey in the honeycomb, and hence He is sweet to our taste as honey dripping from the comb. Sometimes we are so exhausted that we cannot reach out a hand to grasp that honeycomb. And alas, there was a time when our tastes were so depraved that we preferred bitter things and thought them sweet. But now the Holy Ghost has come. We have the honey in the mouth as well as the taste that enjoys it. We have enjoyed it so long that the honey of grace has entered in our nature, and we have become sweet to God, His sweetness having been conveyed to us.

Understanding Jesus' teaching of the role of the Holy Spirit as stated in the text will be approached from three perspectives. First, *what the Holy Spirit does*: "he shall take of mine, and shall show it unto you." Second, *what the Holy Spirit aims at and really effects*: "he shall glorify me." And third, *how in doing both these things He is the Comforter*. We shall find our richest, surest comfort in this work of the Holy Spirit, who takes the things of Christ and shows them to us.

What the Holy Spirit Does

It is clear that the Holy Spirit *deals with the things of Christ*—He does not aim at any originality. All things that Christ had heard from His Father He made known to us. He kept to them. And now the Spirit takes of the things of Christ, and of nothing else. Do not let us strain at anything new. The Holy Ghost could deal with anything in heaven above or in the earth beneath—the story of the ages past, the story of the ages to come, the inward secrets of the earth. He could do it all. Like the Master, He could handle any topic He chose; but He confines Himself to the things of Christ and therein finds unutterable liberty.

Do you think that you can be wiser than His Spirit? And if His choice must be a wise one, will yours be a wise one if you begin to take of the things of something or someone else? You will have the Holy Spirit near you when you are receiving the things of Christ. But, as the Holy Spirit is said never to receive anything else, when you are handling other things, you are handling them alone—the Holy Ghost is not with you there. You may, if you desire, create a theology out of your own vast brain, but the Holy Ghost is not with you there. Resolve to be true to the things of Christ, and you will feel such blessed company with the divine Spirit that you will not envy those who play with a wider range of thoughts.

The Holy Spirit still exists and works and teaches in the church, but we have a test by which to know whether what people claim to be revelation is revelation or not: "he shall receive of mine." The Holy Ghost will never go farther than the cross and the coming of the Lord. He will go no farther than that which concerns Christ. When, therefore, anyone whispers in my ear that such and such has been revealed to him that I do not find in the teaching of Christ and His apostles, I tell him that we must be taught by the Holy Spirit, whose one vocation is to deal with the things of Christ. If we do not remember this, we may be carried away by vagaries, as many have been. Those who explore other things, let them; but as for us, we shall be satisfied to confine our thoughts and our teaching within these limitless limits: "he shall take of mine, and shall show it unto you."

I like to think of how the Holy Spirit handles such things. Those things seem so worthy of Him. They seem so majestic. Now has the Holy Spirit got among the hills. Now is His mighty mind among the infinities when He has to deal with Christ, for Christ is the Infinite veiled in the finite. He seems something more than infinite when He gets into the finite, and the Christ of Bethlehem is less to be understood than the Christ of the Father's bosom. He seems, if it were possible, to have out-infinited the infinite, and the Spirit of God has themes here worthy of His vast nature.

How we waste away dwelling on themes of so little spiritual value! It is in the things of Christ where we need dwell. Oh, imitate the Holy Spirit! If you profess to have Him dwelling in you, be moved by Him. Let it be said of you in your measure, as of the Holy Ghost without measure, "he shall receive of mine, and shall show it unto you."

But what does the Holy Ghost do? *He dwells with us poor creatures*. I can understand the Holy Ghost's taking the things of Christ and rejoicing in them, but the marvel is that the Holy Ghost should glorify Christ by coming and showing these things to us. And yet, it is among us that Christ is to receive His glory. Our eyes must see Him. An unseen Christ is little glorious; and the things of Christ unknown, the things of Christ untasted and unloved, seem to have lost their brilliance to a high degree. The Holy Spirit, therefore, feeling that to show a sinner the salvation of Christ glorifies Him, spends His time, and has been spending these centuries, in taking of the things of Christ and showing them to us. Ah, it is a great condescension on His part to show them to us, but it is a miracle, too! If it were reported that suddenly stones had life and hills had eyes and trees had ears, it would be a strange thing; but for us who were dead and blind and deaf in an awful sense—for the spiritual is more emphatic than the natural—for us to be far gone, and for the Holy Ghost to be able to show the things of Christ to us, is to His honor. But He does do it. He comes from heaven to dwell with us. Let us honor and bless His name.

I am never sure which act of condescension I admire more—the incarnation of Christ or the indwelling of the Holy Ghost. The incarnation of Christ is marvelous—that He should dwell in human nature. But observe, the Holy Ghost dwells in human nature in its sinfulness, not in perfect human nature but in imperfect human nature. And He continues to dwell, not in one body, which was fashioned mysteriously for Himself and was pure and without stain, but He dwells in *our* bodies. These bodies are the temples of the Holy Ghost, bodies that were defiled by sin and in which a measure of defilement remains, despite His indwelling. And this He has done for centuries, not in one instance or in thousands of instances only but in a number that no man can number. He continues still to come into contact with sinful humanity. Not to the angels or to the seraphim does he show the things of Christ, but He shows them to *us*.

It means that *He takes of the words of our Lord*—those that He spoke personally, and those spoken by His apostles. Let us never allow anyone to divide between the word of the apostles and the Word of Christ. Our Savior has joined them together. "Neither pray I for these alone, but for them also which shall believe on me through their word" (John 17:20). And if any begin rejecting the apostolic word, they will be outside the number for whom Christ prays; they shut themselves out by that very fact. I wish that they would solemnly reconsider that the word of the apostles is the Word of Christ. Christ did not remain long enough after the resurrection to give a further exposition of His mind and will; and He could not have given it before His death, because the apostles were not prepared. "I have yet many things to say unto you, but ye cannot bear them now" (John 16:12).

After the descent of the Holy Ghost, the disciples were ready to receive that which Christ spoke by His servants Paul and Peter and James and John. Certain doctrines that we are sometimes taunted about as being revealed not by Christ but by His apostles were all revealed by Christ. They can all be found in Christ's teaching, but they may be in a parabolic form. It is after He has gone up into glory and has prepared a people by His Spirit to understand the truth more fully that He sends His apostles and says, "Go forth, and open up to those whom I have chosen out of the world the meaning of all I said." The meaning is all there, just as all the New Testament is in the Old. Sometimes I have thought that instead of the Old being less inspired than the New, it is more inspired. Things are packed away more tightly in the Old Testament than in the New, if that is possible. There are worlds of meaning in one pregnant line in the Old Testament, and in Christ's words it is just so. Christ is the Old Testament to which the Epistles come in as a kind of New Testament; but the Epistles are all one and indivisible; they cannot be separated.

The words of the Lord Jesus and the words of His apostles are to be *expounded* to us by the Holy Spirit. We shall never get at the center of their meaning apart from His teaching. Even those who wrote them for us did not in many instances fully understand what they wrote. There were some of them who inquired and searched diligently to know what "manner of time the Spirit of Christ which was in them did signify" (1 Pet. 1:11) and of which He had made them speak. And you to whom the words come will have to do the same. You must go and say, "Great Master, thank You for the Book with all my heart, and thank You for putting the Book into words. But now, good Master, I will not dispute over the letter as the Jews did of old, and so miss Your meaning. Open wide the door of the words that I may enter into the secret closet of the meaning, and teach me, I pray. You have the key. Lead me in."

The best way to understand a text of Scripture is to try to read the original. Consult anyone who has studied what the original means, but remember that the quickest way into a text is praying in the Holy Ghost. Pray the chapter over. I do not hesitate to say that if a chapter is read upon one's knees, looking up at every word to Him who gave it, the meaning will come to you with infinitely more light than by any other method of studying it. "He shall glorify me: for he shall receive of mine, and shall show it unto you." He shall redeliver the Master's message to you in the fullness of its meaning.

But that is not all that the text holds: "he shall receive of mine." In the next verse, the Lord goes on to say, "All things that the Father hath are mine." His meaning is that *the Holy Spirit will show us the things of Christ.* Christ speaks as if He had nothing just then that was specially His own, for He had not died then, had not risen, was not yet pleading as the great Intercessor in heaven: all that yet was to come. But still, He says, "Even now all things that the Father hath are mine: all His attributes, His glory, His rest, His happiness, His blessedness. *All that* is mine, and the Holy Ghost shall show that to you."

But that should not limit our text: Christ has indeed died and risen and gone on high; and lo, He comes. His chariots are on the way. There are certain things that the Father has—and that Jesus Christ has—that are truly the things of Christ, emphatically the things of Christ; and my prayer is that you and I might have the text fulfilled in us: "He shall take of mine—my things—and shall show them unto you."

Suppose that I were preparing to preach the Word and the Holy Spirit were to show me our Master in His Godhead. Oh, how I would preach Him as divine—how surely He can bless that message! How certainly He must be able to subdue all things to Himself, seeing that He is very God of very God! It is equally sweet to see Him as man. Oh, to have the Spirit's view of Christ's manhood, distinctly to recognize that He is bone of my bone and flesh of my flesh and that in His infinite tenderness He will compassionate me and deal with my needy people and with the troubled consciences that are around me; that I have only to go to them and tell them of One who is touched with the feeling of their infirmities, having been tempted in all points! Oh, if we once got a view of Christ in His divine and human natures and come down fresh from that vision to speak about Him, what glorious preaching it would be for our people!

It is glorious to get a view of the offices of Christ by the Holy Spirit, but especially of His office as a Savior. I have often said to Him, "You must save my people. It is no business of mine, for I am no savior. But You have learned it by experience, and

You claim it as Your own honor. You are exalted on high to be a Prince and a Savior. Do Your own work, my Lord." May the Holy Ghost show you that Christ is a Savior! A physician does not expect his patients to apologize for their infirmities, and he is trained to help them; so Christ is a Savior, and you need not apologize for going to Him. The fact is that Christ cannot get hold of us anywhere except by our sin. Oh, that the Spirit of God would take of Christ's divine offices, especially that of a Savior, and show them to us!

Did the Holy Ghost ever show you these things of Christ— namely, His covenant agreements? When He struck hands with the Father, it was that He would bring many sons to glory, that of those whom the Father gave Him He would lose none, but that they should be saved, for He is under bonds to His Father to bring His elect home. When the sheep have to pass again under the hand of Him that calls them, they will go under the rod one by one, each one having the mark of blood; and He will never rest till the number in the heavenly fold shall tally with the number in the book. This truth I believe, and what a delight it has been to understand this when I go to preach. On a dull, dreary, wet, foggy morning with only a few present, I believe that God ordained people to be there, and there will be the right number there. I shall preach, and there will be some saved. Guided by the blessed Spirit of God, we go with a living certainty, knowing that God has a people that Christ is bound to bring home, and bring them home He will; and while He shall see of the travail of His soul, His Father shall delight in every one of them. If you get a clear view of that, it will give you backbone and make you strong.

The Holy Ghost favors you by taking what is peculiarly Christ's—namely, His love—and showing it to you. We have seen it, seen it sometimes more vividly than at other times. But if the full blaze of the Holy Spirit were to be concentrated upon the love of Christ and our eyesight enlarged to its utmost capacity, it would be such a vision that heaven could not excel it. We should sit with our Bible before us and feel, "Well, now, here is a man, whether in the body or out of the body I cannot tell. Such a man is caught up into the third heaven." Oh, to see the love of Christ in the light of the Holy Ghost! When it is truly revealed to us, we wonder if we ever understood anything before. The Holy Ghost shows us the naked truth, the essence of the love of Christ; and what that essence is—that love without beginning, without change, without limit, without end; and that love set upon His people simply from motives within Himself—what that must be, what tongue can tell? It is a ravishing sight!

I think that if there could be one sight more wonderful than the love of Christ, it would be the blood of Christ. It is the climax of God. I do not know of anything more divine. It seems to me as if all the eternal purposes worked up to the blood of the cross and then worked from the blood of the cross toward the sublime consummation of all things. To think that He should become man! God has made spirit, pure spirit, embodied spirit, and then materialism. Somehow, as if He would take all up into one, the Godhead links himself with the material; and He wears dust about Him even as we wear it. And taking it all up, He then goes and in that fashion redeems His people from all the evil of their soul, their spirit, and their body by pouring out of a life that, while it was human, was so in connection with the divine that we speak correctly of "the blood of God."

Turn to the twentieth chapter of the Acts and read how the Apostle Paul puts it: "feed the church of God, which he hath purchased with his own blood" (vs. 28). I believe Dr. Watts is not wrong when he says: "God that loved and died." It is an incorrect accuracy—a strictly absolute accuracy of incorrectness. So it must be ever when the finite talks of the Infinite. It was a wonderful sacrifice that could absolutely obliterate, annihilate, and extinguish sin and all traces that could possibly remain of it, for He "came to finish the transgression, and to make an end of sins, and to make reconciliation for iniquity, and to bring in everlasting righteousness" (Dan. 9:24). Have you seen this? You have to see more of it yet. And when we get to heaven, we shall then know what that blood means and with what vigor shall we sing, "Unto him that loved us, and washed us from our sins in his own blood" (Rev. 1:5)!

May the Holy Spirit lead you into Gethsemane, and Golgotha! And then may it please Him to give you a sight of what our Lord is now doing! How it would cheer you up at any time when you were depressed, only to see Him standing and pleading for you! Do you not think that if your wife is ill and your child is sick and times are hard, if you were to see Him with the breastplate on and all the stones glittering, and your name there, and Him pleading for you, you would receive the comfort of the Holy Ghost? And then, to think that He is reigning as well as pleading. He is at the right hand of the Father, who has put all things under His feet. And He waits till the last enemy shall lie there.

Best of all, may the Holy Spirit give you a clear view of His coming. This is our most brilliant hope: "Lo, He cometh!" The more the adversary waxes bold and the less of faith there is, and when zeal seems almost gone, these are the signs of His coming. The Lord always said so, and that He would not come unless there was a falling away first. And so the darker the night grows and the fiercer the storm becomes, the better will we remember that He of the lake of Galilee came to them upon the waves in the night when the storm was wildest. And what will His enemies say when He comes? When they behold the nail prints of the Glorified and the Man with the thorn crown, they who have despised His word and His ever-blessed blood, how will they flee before that face of injured love! And we, on the contrary, through His infinite mercy, will say, "This is what the Holy Ghost showed us; and now we behold it literally. We thank Him for the foresights that He gave us of the marvelous vision."

Remember that when the Holy Ghost takes the things of Christ and shows them to us, He has a purpose in so doing. He says, "Do you see these things? If you can see them, you may have them." Did not Christ Himself say, "Look unto me, and be ye saved, all the ends of the earth" (Isa. 45:22)? Looking gives you a claim, and if you see Him, He is yours. It is with you, with regard to the Spirit showing you things, as it was with Jacob. You know Jacob lay down and went to sleep and the Lord said to Him, "The land whereon thou liest, to thee will I give it" (Gen. 28:13). Now, wherever you go, throughout the whole of Scripture, if you can find a place where you can lie down, that is yours. If you can sleep on a promise, that promise is yours. "Lift up now thine eyes," said God to Abraham, "and look from the place where thou art northward, and southward, and eastward, and westward: for all the land which thou seest, to thee will I give it" (Gen. 13:14–15). The Lord increase our holy vision of delighted faith; for there is nothing you see but you may also enjoy; all that is in Christ is there for you.

What the Holy Spirit Aims at and What He Accomplishes

"He shall glorify me." Ah, the Holy Ghost never comes to glorify *us*, or to glorify a denomination, or, I think, even to glorify a systematic theology. He comes to glorify Christ. If we want to be in accord with Him, we must live and speak in a manner to glorify Christ. Whatever comes into our lives that glorifies self, strike it out ruthlessly. Say, "No, no, no! If it is not distinctly my aim to glorify Christ, I am not obeying the Holy Ghost, and I cannot expect His help."

How, then, does the Holy Spirit glorify Christ? It is very beautiful to think that He glorifies Christ *by showing Christ's things*. If you want to honor someone, you might take him a present. But if you want to glorify Christ, you must go and take the things from Christ's house, "the things of Christ." For instance, whenever we praise God, what do we do? We simply declare what He is. "You are this, and You are that." There is no other praise. We cannot bring anything else to God; the praises of God are simply the facts about Himself. If you want to praise the Lord Jesus Christ, tell the people about Him. Take of the things of Christ and show them to the people, and you glorify Christ. Alas, I know what often happens! Words are weaved together to form and fashion a marvelous and charming piece of literature. If you have done that, put it in the fire and let it burn. It is better to tell what Christ is than to invent ten thousand fine words of praise in reference to Him. "He shall glorify me, for he shall receive of mine, and shall show it unto you."

I think that the blessed Spirit glorifies Christ by showing us the things of Christ *as Christ's*. Oh, to be pardoned! It is a great thing; but to find that pardon in His wounds, that is a greater thing! Oh, to get peace! But to find that peace in the blood of His cross! Brethren, have the blood-mark very visibly on all your mercies. They are all marked with the blood of the cross; but sometimes we think so much of the sweetness of the bread or of the coolness of the waters that we forget where they came from and how they came, and then they lack their choicest flavor. That it came from Christ is the best thing about the best thing that ever came from Christ. That He saves me is somehow better than my being saved. It is a blessed thing to go to heaven; but I do not know that it is not a better thing to be in Christ and so, as the result of it, to get into heaven. It is Himself and that which comes of Himself. So the Holy Ghost shall glorify Christ by making us see that these things of Christ are indeed of Christ and completely of Christ, and still are in connection with Christ; and we enjoy them only because *we* are in connection with Christ.

It is said in the text, "he shall glorify me: for he shall take of mine, and shall show it *unto you.*" Yes, it does glorify Christ for the Holy Spirit to show Christ *to us.* How often I have wished that men of great minds might be converted! I have wished that we could have a few Miltons to sing the love of Christ, a few mighty men who teach politics and the like to consecrate their talents to the preaching of the gospel. Why is it not so? Because the Holy Ghost does not seem to think that that would be the way to glorify Christ supremely; and He prefers, as a better way, to take common people and to take the things of Christ and show them to *us.* He does glorify Christ; and blessed be His name that ever my dim eyes should look upon His infinite loveliness, that ever such a wretch as I, who can understand everything but what I ought to understand, should be made to comprehend the heights and depths and to know with all the saints the love of Christ that passes knowledge. Somehow, it seems our very folly and impotence and spiritual death—if the Holy Ghost shows to us the things of Christ—go toward the increase of that great glorifying of Christ at which the Holy Spirit aims.

Since it is for the honor of Christ for His things to be shown to men, He will show them to us, *that we may go and show them to other people.* This we can do only as He is with us to make the others to see; but He will be with us while we declare what He has taught us, and so the Holy Ghost will really be showing to others while He is showing us. A secondary influence will flow from this service, for we shall be helped to *use the right means* to make others see the things of Christ.

How He Is in Both of These Things Our Comforter

The Holy Spirit is our Comforter, first, for this reason—*there is no comfort like a sight of Christ.* He shows us the things of Christ. If you are poor and the Holy Ghost shows you that Christ had nowhere to lay His head, what a sight for you! If you are sick and the Holy Ghost shows you what sufferings Christ endured, what comfort comes to you! If you are made to see the things of Christ, each thing according to the condition that you are in, how speedily you are delivered out of your sorrow!

And then, if the Holy Ghost glorifies Christ, *that is the cure for every kind of sorrow.* He is the Comforter. Many years ago, after the trauma of the terrible accident in the Surrey Gardens, I had to go into the country and keep quite still. The very sight of the Bible made me cry. I could only keep alone in the garden. I was deeply depressed and sad, for people had been killed in the accident, and there I was, half dead myself. I recall how I got back my comfort. I had been walking around the garden, and I was standing under a tree. If it is there now, I should know that tree; and I remember these words: "Him hath God exalted with His right hand to be a Prince and a Savior." "Oh," I thought to myself, "I am only a common soldier. If I die in a ditch, I do not care. The king is honored. He wins the victory."

I was like those French soldiers in the old times who loved the emperor. You know how, when they were dying, if the emperor rode by, the wounded man would raise himself up on his elbow and cry once more, *"Vive l'Empereur!"* for the emperor was graven on his heart. And so, I am sure, it is with every one of you in this holy war. If our Lord and King is exalted, let other things go which way they like: if He is exalted, never mind what becomes of us. Whatever comes, it is all right if *He* is exalted. God's truth is safe; we are perfectly willing to be forgotten, derided, slandered, or anything else that men please. The King is on the throne. Hallelujah! Blessed be His name!

I would that this rushing mighty wind would come upon His church with an irresistible force that should carry everything before it—the force of truth, but of more than truth, the force of God driving truth home upon the heart and conscience of men. I would that you and I could breathe this wind and receive its invigorating influence, that we might be made champions of God and of His truth. Oh, that it would drive away our mists of doubt and clouds of error. Come, sacred wind, our nation needs You—the whole world requires You. The foul odors that brood over this deadly calm would fly if Your divine lightnings enlightened the world and set the moral atmosphere in commotion. Come, Holy Spirit, come. We can do nothing without You; but if we have Your wind, we spread our sail and speed on toward glory.

Chapter Six

The Superlative Excellence of the Holy Spirit

Nevertheless I tell you the truth; It is expedient for you that I go away: for if I go not away, the Comforter will not come unto you; but if I depart, I will send him unto you—John 16:7.

ALTHOUGH IT IS A DIFFICULT LESSON to learn, the saints of God may very justly count their losses among their greatest gains and their adversities as ministers to their prosperity. Our tendency is to tremble at soul-enriching afflictions, dreading to see those black ships that bring us such freights of golden treasure. When the Holy Spirit sanctifies the furnace, the flame refines our gold and consumes our dross, yet the dull ore of our nature does not like the glowing coals and prefers to lie quiet in the dark mines of earth.

As children cry because they must drink the medicine that will heal their sicknesses, even so do we. Our gracious Savior, however, loves us too wisely to spare us the trouble because of our childish fears. He foresees the advantage that will spring from our griefs and therefore thrusts us into them out of wisdom and true affection. It was very disturbing for the first apostles to lose their Teacher and Friend. Sorrow filled their hearts at the thought that He should depart, yet His departure was to give them the greater blessing of the Holy Spirit, and therefore their entreaties and tears could not avert the dreaded separation. Christ would not gratify their wishes at so great an expense as the withholding of the Spirit. Mourn as they might under the severe trial, Jesus would not remain with them, because His departure was to the highest degree expedient.

God gave two great gifts to His people: the first was *His Son for us;* the second, *His Spirit to us.* After He had given His Son for us, to become incarnate, to work righteousness, and to offer an atonement, that gift had been fully bestowed, and there remained nothing more to do. "It is finished!" proclaimed the completion of the atonement, and His resurrection showed the perfection of justification. It was not therefore necessary that Christ should remain any longer upon earth, since His work was finished.

This is the season for the second gift—the descent of the Holy Spirit. This could not be given until Christ had ascended because this choice favor was reserved to grace with highest honor the triumphant ascension of the great Redeemer. "When he ascended up on high, he led captivity captive, and gave gifts unto men" (Eph. 4:8). This was the great promise that Jesus received of His Father. "Therefore being by the right hand of God exalted, and having received of the Father the promise of the Holy Ghost, he hath shed forth this, which ye now see and hear" (Acts 2:33). That His triumphal entrance into heaven might be stamped with signal glory, the gifts of the Spirit of God could not be scattered among the sons of men until the ascension.

The first gift being completed, it became necessary that He whose person and work make up that priceless treasure should withdraw Himself that He might have power to distribute the second benefit by which alone the first gift becomes of any service to us. Christ crucified is of no practical value to us without the work of the Holy Spirit, and the atonement can never save a single soul unless the blessed Spirit of God applies it to the heart and conscience. Jesus is never seen until the Holy Spirit opens the eye; the water from the well of life is never received until the Holy Spirit has drawn it from the depths. As medicine remains unused pending the physician's word, as sweets go untasted because they are out of reach, as treasure lies unvalued because it is hidden in the earth—such is Jesus the Savior until the Holy Spirit teaches us to know Him.

It is to the honor of the Holy Spirit that I humbly consider this theme, and may the same hallowed flame that of old sat upon the apostles now rest upon the writer, and may the Word come with power to your heart.

The Physical Presence of Christ Must Have Been Exceedingly Precious

How precious was Christ can be told only by those who love Him much. Love always desires to be in the company of the thing beloved, and absence causes grief. What is fully meant by the expression "Sorrow hath filled your heart" only those who anticipate a similar painful bereavement can know. Jesus had become the joy of their eyes, the sun of their days, the star of their nights: like the spouse, as she came up from the wilderness, they leaned upon their beloved. They were as little children, and now that their Lord and Master was going, they felt like orphans. Well might they have great sorrow of heart. So much love, so much sorrow, when the object of love is withdrawn.

Consider the joy that the physical presence of Christ would give to us, and then you can tell how precious it must be. Have we not personally been longing for and expecting Jesus to return in His second coming? This is the bright hope that cheers the Christian—the hope that the Savior shall descend to reign among His people gloriously. Imagine Him appearing suddenly right where you are, how would you clap your hands! The lame would leap like a hart, and even the dumb might sing for joy. The presence of the Master! What rapture! Come quickly! Come quickly, Lord Jesus!

It must be indeed a precious thing to enjoy the physical presence of Christ. Think of the advantage it would be in the teaching of His people. No mystery need puzzle us if we could refer all questions to Him. The disputes of the church would soon be ended, for He would tell us what His Word meant beyond dispute. There would be no discouragement to the church in her service of faith and labor of love, for the presence of Christ would be the end of all difficulties and would insure conquest over all enemies. What a delightful thing to know that Christ was somewhere upon earth, for then He would take the personal supervision of His universal church. He would warn us of apostates; He could reject the hypocrites; He would comfort the weak and rebuke the erring. How delightful it would be to see Him walking among the golden candlesticks, holding the stars in His right hand. Christ would create unity, and heresy would be rooted out. The presence of Jesus, whose countenance is as the sun shining in his strength, would ripen all the fruits of our garden, consume all the weeds, and quicken every plant. The two-edged sword of His mouth would slay His foes, and His eyes of fire would kindle the holy passions of His friends.

But I shall not enlarge upon that point, because it is one in which imagination exercises itself at the expense of judgment. I question whether the church is yet prepared to enjoy the physical presence of her Savior without falling into the error of knowing Him after the flesh. It may be centuries before the church is ready to see her Savior in the flesh on earth again, because I see in my own self—as I suppose it is so in you—that much of the delight that I expect from the company of Christ is according to the sight of the eyes and the judgment of the mind, and sight is ever the mark and symbol of the flesh.

The Presence of the Comforter Is Much Better Than the Physical Presence of Christ

We have imagined that the bodily presence of Christ would make us blessed and confer innumerable gifts; but according to our text, the presence of the Holy Ghost working in the church is more necessary for the church. If you think for a moment, the physical presence of Christ on the earth, however good it might be for the church, would in our present condition involve many inconveniences that are avoided by His presence through the Holy Spirit. Christ, being most truly man, must as to His manhood inhabit a certain place. Thus, to get to Christ, it would be necessary for us to travel to His place of residence. Imagine everyone in the world having to travel from the ends of the earth to visit the Lord Jesus Christ in the city of Jerusalem. While all might joyfully make the journey, yet as they could not all live where they could every morning see Christ, they must be content with every now and then getting a glimpse of Him. But the Holy Spirit dwells everywhere, and if we wish to apply to the Holy Spirit, we have no need to move an inch. Jesus Christ could be present in only one congregation in the world, but the Holy Spirit is everywhere. Through the Holy Spirit, Christ keeps His promise, "For where two or three are gathered together in my name, there am I in the midst of them" (Matt. 18:20). Christ could not keep that promise according to the flesh; but through the Holy Spirit, we sweetly enjoy His presence and hope to do so until the world's end.

Imagine the difficulty of gaining access to Christ. There are only twenty-four hours in the day, and if our Lord never slept, what are twenty-four hours for the supervision of a church that covers the earth? How could millions of believers all receive immediate personal comfort, either from His lips or from the smiles of His face? What could one man do by His personal presence, even though that one man were incarnate Deity? What could He do in one day for the comfort of all of these? We could hardly expect to have our turn once in the year. But we can now see Jesus every hour and every moment of every hour. As often as you bow the knee, His Spirit can commune with you and bless you. Wherever and whenever, the Spirit waits to be gracious, and your sighs and cries climb up to Christ in heaven and return with answers of peace. The presence of the Spirit makes Christ accessible to every saint at all times. Not to a few choice favorites, but to every believing man and woman, the Holy Ghost is always accessible.

We should consider that Christ's presence in the flesh upon the earth would involve another difficulty. Of course, since every word that Christ would have spoken from the time of the apostles until now would have been inspired, busy scribes would be always taking down Christ's words. If in the short course of three years our Savior managed to do and say so much that one of the Evangelists informs us that if all had been written, the world itself could not have contained the books that would have been written, I ask you to imagine what a mass of literature the church would have acquired if she had preserved *all* the words of Christ. The Word of God would have consisted of innumerable volumes of the sayings and deeds of the Lord Jesus Christ. Not even the studious could have read all the Lord's teachings. But now we have a book that is finished within a narrow compass with not another line to be added to it. The canon of revelation is sealed up forever; and the poorest believer, going with a humble soul to that book and looking up to Jesus Christ, may comprehend the doctrines of grace and understand with all saints what are the heights and depths and know the love of Christ that passes knowledge. So then, as precious as the physical presence of Christ might be, it is infinitely better for the church's good that Christ should be present by His Spirit.

Yet more, if Jesus Christ were still present with His church in the flesh, *the life of faith* would not have such room. The more there is visible to the eye, the less room for faith; the least faith the most show. The more faith grows, the less it needs outward helps; and when faith shows her true character and is divorced from sense and sight, she wants absolutely nothing to rest upon but the invisible power of God. Faith rests upon the invisible pillars of God's truth and faithfulness, needing nothing to shore or buttress her. The presence of Christ Jesus here in bodily flesh would be the bringing back of the saints to the life of sight and, in a measure, would spoil the simplicity of naked trust. You remember the Apostle Paul says, "Henceforth know we no man after the flesh: yea, though we have known Christ after the flesh, yet now henceforth know we him no more" (2 Cor. 5:16).

To the skeptic who should ask us, "Why do you believe in Christ?," if Jesus had remained upon the earth, we could always give an easy answer: "There He is." There would be very little room for faith's holy adherence to the Word of God and no opportunity for her to glorify God. But now, the fact that we have nothing visible to point to that carnal minds can understand makes the path of faith more truly congenial with its noble character. "Faith, mighty faith, the promise sees, and looks to that alone," which she could hardly do if she could look upon the visible person of a present Savior. What a happy day it will be when faith enjoys the full fruition of her hopes in the triumphant advent of her Lord; but His absence alone can train and educate her to the needed point of spiritual refinement.

Furthermore, the presence of Jesus Christ on earth would materially affect the character of God's great battle against error and sin. Suppose that persecuting tyrants had their arms dried up or that all men who opposed Christ were suddenly devoured by fire. It would be a battle between physical greatness and moral evil—a warfare in which only spiritual force is employed on the side of right. But now that Christ has gone, the fight is all between spirit and spirit, between the Holy Spirit and Satan, between truth and error, between the earnestness of believers and the infatuation of unbelievers. Now the fight is fair. We have no miracle on our side—the Holy Spirit is enough. We call no fire from heaven; no earthquake shakes the ground beneath our foe's feet. Physical force is left to our enemies; we do not ask for it. Why? Because by the divine working, we can vanquish error without it. In the name of the Holy One of Israel, in whose cause we have been enlisted—by *His* might we are enough, without miracles and signs and wonders. The absence of the physical Savior makes it a spiritual conflict of spirit of the noblest and sublimest order.

Only this one further remark—that the personal presence of Christ did not produce very great results in His disciples until the Spirit was poured forth from on high. Christ was their Teacher—how much did they learn? There is Philip—Christ has to say to him, "Have I been so long time with you, and yet hast thou not known me, Philip?" (John 14:9). The disciples were puzzled by questions that little children can now answer. You can see that at the end of their three years of training with Christ they had made but slender progress. Christ is not only their Teacher but also their Comforter, yet how frequently Christ could not console them because of their unbelief. After giving that delightful discourse that we have been reading, He found them sleeping for sorrow. In this very chapter, when He is trying to comfort them, He adds, "But because I have said these things unto you, sorrow hath filled your heart" (John 16:6). Christ's object was to foster the graces of His disciples, but where are their graces? Here is Peter—he has not even the grace of courage and consistency but denies his Master while the rest forsake and fly. Even then the Spirit of Christ was not infused into the disciples. They scarcely knew the truths that their Master taught, and they were far enough from imbibing His heavenly Spirit.

Even the disciples' endowments were slender. It is true they once worked miracles and preached, but with what success? Do you ever hear of Peter winning three thousand sinners under a sermon till the Holy Spirit came? Even the ministry of our Lord Jesus Christ, considered only as to its immediate fruits, was not to be compared with ministries after the descent of the Spirit. "He came unto his own, and his own received him not" (John 1:11). His great work as a Redeemer was a complete triumph from beginning to end; but as a Teacher, since the Spirit of God was only upon *Him* and not upon the people, His words were rejected, His entreaties were despised, and His warnings unheeded by the great multitudes. The mighty blessing came when the words of Joel were fulfilled: "And it shall come to pass afterward, that I will pour out my spirit upon all flesh; and your sons and your daughters shall prophesy, your old men shall dream dreams, your young men shall see visions: And also upon the servants and upon the handmaids in those days will I pour out my spirit" (Joel 2:28–29). That was the blessing so rich and so rare that it was indeed expedient that Jesus Christ should go that the Holy Spirit might descend.

The Presence of the Comforter Is Superlatively Valuable

While the presence of Christ was most precious, the presence of the Holy Spirit is clearly shown to be of more practical value for the church. Consider, then, that the presence of the Comforter is superlatively valuable. We may gather this first from the effects that were seen upon the day of Pentecost. On the day of Pentecost, the Holy Spirit sounded the alarm of war. The soldiers were hardly prepared for it; they were a frail group, having only this virtue—that they were content to wait until power was given to them. They sat still in the upper room. That mighty sound was heard across Jerusalem and filled the place where they were sitting. Here was a prediction of what the Spirit of God was to be to the church.

The Holy Spirit is to come mysteriously upon the church according to the sovereign will of God; but when He comes like the wind, it is to purge the moral atmosphere and to quicken the pulse of all who breathe spiritually. This is a blessing indeed, a treasure that the church greatly needs. I would that this rushing mighty wind would come upon His church with an irresistible force that should carry everything before it—the force of truth, but of more than truth, the force of God driving truth home upon the heart and conscience of men. I would that you and I could breathe this wind and receive its invigorating influence, that we might be made champions of God and of His truth. Oh, that it would drive away our mists of doubt and clouds of error. Come, sacred wind, our nation needs You—the whole world requires You. The foul odors that brood over this deadly calm would fly if Your divine lightnings enlightened the world and set the moral atmosphere in commotion. Come, Holy Spirit, come. We can do nothing without You; but if we have Your wind, we spread our sail and speed on toward glory.

Then the Spirit came as fire. A fire-shower accompanied the rushing mighty wind. What a blessing this is to the church! The church needs fire to inspire her ministers, to give zeal and energy to all her members. Having this fire, she burns her way to success. The world meets her with an evil fire, but she confronts the world with the fire of souls aglow with the love of Jesus Christ. She trusts not the eloquence and wisdom of her preachers, but trusts to the divine fire that clothes them with energy. She knows that men are irresistible when they are filled with hallowed enthusiasm sent from God. Her cry is, "Come, holy fire, abide upon our pastors and teachers! Rest upon every one of us!" This fire is a blessing Christ did not bring us in person, but one that He now gives through His Spirit to the church.

Then there came from the fire-shower a descent of tongues. This, too, is the privilege of the church. When the Lord gave the apostles various tongues, He did, as it were, give them the keys of the various kingdoms. "Go," He said, "Judea is not my only dominion, go and unlock the gates of every empire, here are the keys, you can speak every language." Although we can no longer speak with every man in his own tongue, we have the keys of the whole world if we have the Spirit of God with us. You have the keys of human hearts if the Spirit of God speaks through you. There is power about the gospel, when the Spirit is with us, little dreamed of by those who call it the foolishness of men. I am persuaded that the results that have followed the ministry in our lifetime are trivial and insignificant compared with what they would be if the Spirit of God were more mightily at work. There is no reason, in the nature of the gospel or the power of the Spirit, why a whole congregation should not be converted under one sermon. The success given on the day of Pentecost was only the first fruits, not the harvest. We have been accustomed to look on Pentecost as a great and wonderful display of divine power not to be equalled again. Believe me, it is to be exceeded. I stand not upon Pentecost as upon a towering mountain, wondering at my height, but I look at Pentecost as a little rising knoll from which I am to look up to mountains that are far loftier. You must expect greater things, pray for greater things, long for greater things. Here is our nation, sunk in stolid ignorance of the gospel. How is she to be made sober and sanctified to God? "Not by might, nor by power, but by my spirit, saith the LORD of hosts." Where is the sword that shall find her heart? "Not by might, nor by power, but by my spirit, saith the LORD of hosts" (Zech. 4:6).

The one thing, then, that we need is the Spirit of God. Do not say that we need money; we shall have it soon enough when the Spirit touches men's hearts. Do not say that we need buildings, churches, and programs. All these have their place, but the main need of the church is the Spirit and men into whom the Spirit may be poured. If there were only one prayer that I might pray before I die, it should be this: "Lord, send Your church men filled with the Holy Ghost and with fire." Give to any denomination such men, and its progress will be mighty. Send it college gentlemen of great refinement but of little fire and grace, and straightway that denomination must decline. The preacher may be rustic, simple, and unmannered, but if the Holy Ghost is upon him, none of his adversaries shall stand against him; his word shall be with power to the shaking of the gates of hell. Did I not say that the Spirit of God is of superlative importance to the church and that the day of Pentecost seems to tell us this?

Here is another thought that should make the Spirit very dear to you—that without the Holy Spirit, no good thing ever did or ever can come into your heart—no sigh of repentance, no cry of faith, no glance of love, no tear of hallowed sorrow. Your heart can never beat with life divine except by the Spirit. You are not capable of the smallest degree of spiritual emotion, much less spiritual action, apart from the Holy Ghost. You were absolutely dead for God until the Holy Ghost came and raised you from the grave. There is nothing good in you today that was not put there. The flowers of Christ are all exotics—"In me, that is, in my flesh, dwelleth no good thing" (Rom. 7:18). "Who can bring a clean thing out of an unclean? not one" (Job 14:4). Everything must come from Christ, and Christ gives nothing to men except through the Spirit of all grace. Prize, then, the Spirit as the channel of all good that comes to you.

Further, no good thing can come out of you apart from the Spirit. It may be in your life, yet it lies dormant unless God works in you to will and to do of His own good pleasure. Do you desire to preach? How can you unless the Holy Ghost touches your tongue? Do you desire to pray? Alas, what dull work it is unless the Spirit makes intercession for you! Do you desire to conquer sin? Would you be holy? Do you desire to rise to superlative heights of spirituality? Are you wanting to be full of zeal and ardor for the Master's cause? You cannot without the Spirit— "Without me ye can do nothing." O branch of the vine, you can have no fruit without the sap! O child of God, you have no life apart from the life that God gives you through His Spirit! Did I not say that the Holy Spirit is superlatively precious?

Conclusion

If these things are so, let us view the mysterious Spirit with deep awe and reverence. Let us so reverence Him as not to grieve or provoke Him to anger by our sin. Let us not quench Him in one of His faintest motions in our soul. Let us foster every suggestion and be ready to obey every prompting. If the Holy Spirit is indeed so mighty, let us do nothing without Him. Let us begin no project and carry on no enterprise and conclude no transaction without seeking His blessing. Tremble in His presence, put off your shoes, for the place where you stand is holy ground. Let us confess our entire weakness apart from Him and then, depending upon Him alone, have this as our prayer, "Open my heart and my whole being to Your incoming, and uphold me with Your free spirit when I shall have received that spirit in my inward being."

In the next place, as a practical remark, let us take courage today. When we look at the great ones of the earth, we see them on the side of the false and not of the truth. Where are the kings and mighty men? Are they not against the Lord of Hosts? Where are the gold and silver, architecture, wisdom, and eloquence? Are they not banded against the Lord of Hosts? What then! Shall we be discouraged? Our fathers were not. They bore their testimony in the stocks and in the prisons, but they refused to fear. Like John Bunyan, they learned to rot in dungeons, but they did not learn to play the coward. They suffered, and they testified that they were not discouraged. Why? Because they knew that the Spirit of God is mighty and will prevail. Better to have a small church of poor men and the Spirit of God with them than to have a heirarchy of kings without the Holy Spirit, for this is not merely the cord of strength, but it is strength itself. Where the Spirit of God is, there is liberty and power.

We have only to seek for that which God has promised to give, and we can do wonders. God will give the Holy Spirit to them who ask. Wake up to earnest prayer. Cry aloud to God to let His bare arm be seen. Learn the power of prayer. Give the Covenant Angel no rest till He speaks the word and the Spirit works mightily among the sons of men. Prayer is work adapted to each of you who are in Christ. You may not preach or teach, but you can pray, and your private prayer, unknown to men, shall be registered in heaven. Those silent but earnest cries of yours shall bring down a blessing. I love to hear friends praying with the groaning that cannot be uttered, "Lord, send the Spirit! Send the Spirit, Lord! Work! Work! Work!"

I am persuaded we only need more prayer, constant prayer, Spirit-led prayer, and there would be no limit to the blessing. Cry aloud and spare not. Give Him no rest till He sends His Spirit once again to stir the waters and brood over this dark world till light and life shall come. Cry day and night, O ye elect of

God, for He will answer you speedily. The time of battle draws near. Now for the sword of the Lord and of Gideon! Now for the old might and majesty of ancient days! Now for the shaking of the walls of Jericho, even though we have no better weapons than rams' horns! Now for the coming of the Holy Spirit with such might and power that as Noah's flood covered the mountain tops, Jehovah's flood of glory shall cover the highest summits of sin and iniquity, and the Lord God Omnipotent shall reign over the whole world.

I do not believe the Spirit of God desires us to live with only salvation's essentials. There are miserable souls who obey and love no more than is absolutely needful to get to heaven. They would be saved in the cheapest possible way, and they would be content to crawl over the threshold of glory, but not to go too far in. They want as much grace as may be necessary to float them into the harbor, but they do not desire an abundant entrance. O miserly professors, I turn to the children of God and joyfully remind them that there is in the Holy Ghost not only what they absolutely need to be saved but also much more. Here is not only bread but also wine on the lees well refined. In the Holy Ghost there is comfort to gladden you, grace to strengthen you, holiness to ennoble you, and love to purify you.

Chapter Seven

Receiving the Holy Ghost

Have ye received the Holy Ghost since ye believed?—Acts 19:2.

IT IS INTERESTING TO NOTE in Paul's question to the Ephesian disciples of John what he did *not* ask them. He did not say, "Have ye believed?" This would have been an important question, and one that should be easily answered. Our faith must be either boldly affirmed or sorrowfully denied, but it should not remain the subject of question. It is a great pity that so many Christians allow that question to remain a matter of debate, for as long as the existence of faith within our souls is in question, we must remain unhappy. Faith is the cornerstone of the edifice of godliness, and if it is not well laid, there can be no sense of security to the inhabitant of the house. We should know not only what we believe but also to whom we believe; and it is of great importance that we advance beyond common believing to the full assurance of faith, hope, and understanding.

Again, Paul does not put the question, "If ye believed, how was faith created in your souls? When did you first become believers?" These are interesting questions, but they do not touch the essence of salvation. A man may be saved and yet know none of the details of his conversion. No doubt, there are many strong believers who could not point to any special event or means by which faith was born within them. In general, faith came by the hearing of the Word of God and the operation of the Holy Spirit; but those believers do not remember, as some do, a remarkable text or thrilling sermon or striking providence through which they were turned from darkness to light. Thousands in the fold of Jesus came back to the good Shepherd by degrees. Many who now walk in the light received daylight, not by the leaping of the sun above the horizon in a moment but as our days usually begin: a little light tinged the eastern sky, and then came a rosy hue, followed by a dim dawn; and afterward came the actual rising of the sun out its chambers of the east, and the sun runs his course till he has created perfect day. Many are gradually brought to Christ, and yet they are truly brought to Christ.

Paul does ask, "Have ye received the Holy Ghost since ye believed?" The Revised Version reads it, "Did ye receive the Holy Ghost when ye believed?" Others that are probably quite as accurate read it, "Are ye receiving the Holy Ghost now that ye have believed?" All the renderings really come to this: Do you see a connection between your believing and the Holy Ghost? Did you receive Him when you believed? Have you received Him since you believed? Are you daily receiving Him as you believe? That is the subject before us—the Holy Spirit in our hearts as believers. Has your faith been sealed by the impress of the Holy Ghost? This is a point of utmost importance expressed by the apostle with deep and solemn earnestness in the power of the Holy Spirit.

When the Holy Spirit was given at Pentecost, He showed His presence by certain miraculous signs. Some of those who received the Holy Spirit spoke with tongues, others began to prophesy, and others received gifts of healing. I am sure that if these were given now in connection with the reception of the Holy Spirit, you would be anxious to possess them. You would want to be healing, or speaking in tongues, or working miracles by which you could benefit others and glorify God.

It should not be forgotten that those works of the Holy Spirit that are permanent are of greater value than those that are transitory. We cannot suppose that the Holy Ghost brought forth the best wine at first and that His operations gradually deteriorated. It is a rule of the kingdom to keep the best wine to the last;

therefore I conclude that the works of the Holy Spirit that are operating in the church today are every way as valuable as those earlier miraculous gifts. The work of the Holy Spirit, by which men are quickened from their death in sin, is not inferior to the power that made men speak in tongues. His work of comforting men and making them glad in Christ is by no means second to the opening of the eyes of the blind. Men might have the gifts of the Spirit as to miracles, and yet perish after all; but he who has the spiritual gifts of the Holy Ghost will never perish: they are saving blessings, and where they come, they lift the man out of his sinful estate and make him a child of God. I would therefore seriously inquire whether you have received these more permanent gifts of the Spirit that are today open to all, by which you shall work no physical miracle but shall receive spiritual wonders of a grander sort.

Have you, then, received the Spirit since you believed? Are you now receiving the Spirit? Are you living under His divine influence? Are you filled with His power? Put the question personally. I am afraid many believers will have to admit that they hardly know whether there is a Holy Ghost. Others will confess that though they have enjoyed a little of His saving work, they know almost nothing of His empowering and sanctifying influence. Few of us have participated in His operations as we might have: we have sipped where we might have drunk; we have drunk where we might have bathed; we have bathed up to the ankles where we might have found rivers to swim in. Alas, Jesus' words concerning many Christians must be affirmed—that they have been naked and poor and miserable when they might in the power of the Holy Spirit have been clad in golden garments and have been rich and increased in goods. The Holy Spirit waits to be gracious, but we linger in indifference, like those of whom we read, "They could not enter in because of unbelief" (Heb. 3:19). Therefore, I press home the apostle's question, "Have ye received the Holy Ghost since ye believed?"

The Apostle's Question

In some respects, it is *a vital question*. It does not play about the outskirts of religion but plunges into its very center. The question has nothing to do with the church affiliation to which you belong; it is an inquiry that touches the heart of the man and the inmost life of man's spirit. "Have ye received the Holy Ghost since ye believed?" For, remember, the Holy Ghost is the author of all spiritual *life*. Life does not lie latent in natural men for themselves to stir up, but until the Holy Spirit visits them, men are dead in their trespasses and sins. If, when you believed, there was not the impartation of life by the Holy Spirit, your believing was a dead believing, the mere counterfeit of living faith. If the Holy Ghost has not been with you since your conversion, every act of your religion has been formal, dead, and unaccepted. In vain have you tuned your formal songs; in vain have you attempted to adore; your Hosannahs have languished on your tongue, and your devotion has fallen like a corpse before the altar. If the Holy Ghost is not there, life is not there: your prayers have been a mockery; your joys have been delusions; your griefs have been carnal. That which is born of the flesh is flesh, and nothing better. Only that which is born of the Spirit is spirit. There must, then, be a work from heaven, a work of the Holy Ghost upon the heart, or else you have not believed unto life, and you remain in death.

As the Holy Ghost is the Author of spiritual life, so is He the Author of all true *instruction*. You have professed to be a believer, but you know nothing at all unless the Holy Spirit has taught you. "All thy children shall be taught of the LORD" (Isa. 54:13). To be taught of the minister is nothing, but to be taught of the Lord is everything. It is only the Spirit of God who can engrave the truth upon the fleshy tablets of the heart. We speak to the ear, but only He can speak to the inmost soul. He who has never received the truth in the power of it, as delivered by the Spirit of light and fire, has need to begin again and learn the basics of the faith. The knowledge of the letter only puffs up those who rest in it, and eventually the letter kills; but the inward whisper, the secret admonition, the silent operation of the Spirit of God that falls as the dew from heaven upon the heart—this is quite another thing. Without it we are blind and ignorant, though we may be esteemed a theologian. We are still in the dark unless the Spirit of God has shone in upon our soul.

Furthermore, if we have believed in Christ, the Holy Ghost

has come upon us to *transform* us altogether. By divine grace we are not now what we used to be: we have new thoughts, new wishes, new aspirations, new sorrows, new joys, and they are worked in us by the Spirit. A man's believing is nothing unless he is made to be a new creature in Christ Jesus. But how can we be made new by any power than the Holy Spirit? Only He that creates can new-create. "Except a man be born again, he cannot see the kingdom of God" (John 3:3). We cannot hate evil and love ourselves correctly, for the whole bent and bias of our spirit since the fall are toward evil, only evil, and that continually. Neither can we renew ourselves. Who can bring a clean thing out of an unclean? The Holy Spirit must transform us by the renewing of our minds: we must be "begotten again unto a lively hope by the resurrection of Jesus Christ from the dead" (1 Pet. 1:3). If our faith has not brought with it the Holy Spirit, if it is not the fruit of the Spirit and we are not changed in nature and in life, our faith is presumption and our profession is a lie.

Furthermore, it is absolutely essential that we should be *sanctified*. A faith that does not work for purification will work for putrefaction. Unless our faith makes us hunger for holiness and pant after conformity to God, it is no better than the faith of devils, and perhaps it is not even that good. How can anyone become holy except by the Spirit of holiness? A holy man is the workmanship of the Holy Spirit. Through faith we are sanctified by the operation of the Holy Ghost, so that we are delivered from the dominion of sin and set free to follow after that which is good and pure and right in the sight of God. Faith that does not bring holiness will never bring us into communion with the living God. Oh, the absolute necessity that the Holy Ghost should rest upon us!

Besides that, remember, there is one mark of God's people which if it is lacking is fatal, and that is *prayer*. "Behold, he prayeth," is a true sign of the new birth; but can a man pray without the assistance of the Holy Spirit? Let him try to do so, and if he is honest, he will soon find the value of the verse: "Likewise the Spirit also helpeth our infirmities: for we know not what we should pray for as we ought: but the Spirit itself maketh intercession for us with groanings which cannot be uttered" (Rom. 8:26). Pray without the Spirit of God? It will be a mechanical performance, the statue of prayer, but not the living, prevailing supplication of an heir of heaven. Unless you invoke the Holy Spirit, the exercise shall be heartless and the results worthless. What is the incense without the burning coals? What is the mercy seat without the Shekinah light? Prayer without the Spirit is as a bird without wings, an arrow without a bow. You will leave your time of prayer unrefreshed if you have been without the Spirit. Even the desire to pray must be born by the Holy Ghost; no true word of supplication can arise from the heart unless the Spirit of God prompts it.

Do you not see how essential the Holy Spirit is to spiritual life? If all you have is what you have made yourself, you and your works must perish. If your prayers have risen from no greater depth than your own heart and if they are the fruit of no better spirit than your own, they will never reach the ear of God. If there is nothing supernatural about your religion, it will be a millstone about your neck to sink you into hell. What comes from the dunghill and is of the dunghill will rot on the dunghill. That which comes from above will elevate a man to its own element and cause him to dwell with Christ at the right hand of God.

But now, while this is a vital question, I beg to say further that *where it is not vital, it is nevertheless greatly important.* I do not believe the Spirit of God desires us to live with only salvation's essentials. There are miserable souls who obey and love no more than is absolutely needful to get to heaven. They would be saved in the cheapest possible way, and they would be content to crawl over the threshold of glory, but not to go too far in. They want as much grace as may be necessary to float them into the harbor, but they do not desire an abundant entrance. O miserly professors, I turn to the children of God and joyfully remind them that there is in the Holy Ghost not only what they absolutely need to be saved but also much more. Here is not only bread but also wine on the lees well refined. In the Holy Ghost there is comfort to gladden you, grace to strengthen you, holiness to ennoble you, and love to purify you.

The Spirit of God is the *Comforter*, and how important it is that you be comforted! Why do you hang your head? Why do you mourn as if you were in the night and the dews were thick upon your eyelids? You are the child of the morning, and the child of the day. Rejoice in the Lord and walk in the light as He is in the light. "Have ye received the Holy Ghost since ye believed?" You whose brows are furrowed with care, whose hearts are distracted with anxiety, receive the Spirit of consolation and be glad in the Lord, for the joy of the Lord is your strength.

In the Holy Ghost there is also a spirit of *enlightening*. Do you read the Word of God and yet understand little of it? Why is this? Should you not seek more of the teaching of the Holy Spirit that He may lead you into all truth? How much happier you would be, and how much more effective if you knew more of the things of God! The Holy Spirit can take of the things of Christ and show them to you. Now you only see men as trees walking, but there is no need to be content with such dim vision, for the Comforter can anoint your eyes with salve that you may see, He can open your eyes that you may behold wondrous things out of His law. Why not seek the enlightening of the Spirit of God to teach you His Word and way?

The Spirit of God is also the spirit of *liberty*, but some of God's children do not seem to have yet attained their freedom. They have one shackle remaining on their foot, and though they try to enter the broad fields of heavenly enjoyment, they cannot escape their prison. Of such we may well ask, "Have ye received the Holy Ghost since ye believed?" If so, why are you the slaves of tradition? Why do you ask permission of others to breathe and think spiritually? Why are you so cowardly that you dare not follow conscience or speak the things of God?

The fear of man brings a snare to many, and that snare is also a chain to the feet. It should not be so. Rather, men should feel that since the Son has made them free, they are free indeed. The Holy Spirit is a free Spirit and makes men free; where the Spirit of the Lord is, there is liberty. Glory be to You, O God, "I am thy servant; thou hast loosed my bonds." Many weak children of God have received the spirit of bondage again to fear, but they have not yet received the Spirit of adoption by which we cry, "Abba, Father." Oh, the glory of the Spirit of God when He makes us feel that we are no more servants but sons, not under law but grace, not under wrath but love, not doomed to death but endowed with life! He has broken our bonds asunder. He has set our feet in a large room and made us to walk at liberty because we keep His statutes. Ours is the freedom of the heavenly citizenship, and it is important we know what this freedom means.

Some Christians need to feel the Spirit of God as a power *moving and impelling them to holy service.* Do you never hear a voice behind you saying, "This is the way; walk ye in it"? Have you never known holy impulses bidding you do this and that—impulses that did not come from human nature, for they caused you to do something that you would naturally have avoided? And do you never follow after things unseen, driven onward as by a powerful wind? Have you not been made willing, in the day of God's power, to do the divine bidding?

That same Spirit who moves the saints to service also *empowers* them to achieve the purpose that is put into their hearts. By His aid you shall go forth in your feebleness and put to flight the armies of the enemy. You shall be in God's hand as a sharp threshing instrument having teeth and shall thresh mountains, yes, fan them, and the wind shall carry them away. Does any man know what the Spirit of God can make of him? I believe the greatest, ablest, most faithful, most holy man of God might have been greater, abler, more faithful, and more holy if he had put himself more completely at the Spirit's disposal. Wherever God has done great things by a man, He has had power to do more had the man been ready for it. We are limited in ourselves, not in God. The church is weak today because the Holy Spirit is not upon her members as we could desire Him to be. We totter along like feeble babes, whereas had we more of the Spirit, we might walk without fainting, run without weariness, and even mount up with wings as eagles. Oh, for more of the anointing of the Holy Ghost whom Christ is prepared to give immeasurably if we will but receive Him! "Have ye received the Holy Ghost since ye believed?" Is there not much divine power that has not been manifested in you?

"Oh," you say, "I feel so dull today!" Is not the Holy Spirit the power to refresh and rekindle in your soul the dying flame of spiritual fervor? If you received His power, you would not mind the heaviness of the atmosphere or any other deadening surroundings, for the Spirit would triumph over the flesh. Do you know the power of the Spirit? Did you never run like Elijah before Ahab's chariot and feel that it was a small thing to do?

Can you not say, "O my soul, you have trodden down strength! By my God I have leaped over a wall and broken through a troop: I can do all things through Christ that strengtheneth me"? These are the expressions of souls familiar with the Holy Ghost. Are you receiving His fullness even now?

Now I come to notice that *this question is assuredly answerable.* "Have ye received the Holy Ghost since ye believed?" The idea has sprung up that you cannot answer this, but you can. Give someone an electric shock and I guarantee he will know it, but if he has the Holy Ghost, he will know it much more. We cannot live on guesswork as to our daily life, much less as to eternal things. Live daily on what God gives you, and you cannot doubt. Live near to Christ, and you cannot doubt whether you love Him. Live in the Holy Spirit, give yourselves up fully to His divine anointings, and you will not say, "I hardly know whether there *is* a Holy Ghost," for He dwells with you and shall be in you.

Permit me to say here that there are many believers to whom *this question is inevitable.* I pick out certain of them. There is the brother with the long dreary face—the Knight of the Rueful Countenance. You know him, and you pity him. His favorite hymn is "'Tis a point I long to know, Oft it causes anxious thought." He delights in things dreary as much as he can delight in anything. He is sure of nothing but the horrible: everything that is pleasant he is afraid of. His life is one protracted groan. Come along and please tell me, "Have ye received the Holy Ghost since ye believed?" How he hesitates! Poor soul, he is perplexed. He is not well acquainted with the Comforter. Surely, if we have the Spirit, we ought to rejoice in the Lord always. How is this when the Comforter has come to you?

Another brother is a member of the church and a very unpleasant neighbor, for he picks holes in everybody and everything. He is a born grumbler, and his new birth has not changed the habit. You who are so uneasy and unhappy, so worrying and annoying to everybody, did you receive the Holy Ghost when you believed? I have sometimes thought, from the sharp acid of their temperament that certain unhappy friends must have been baptized in vinegar instead of water. Surely the Spirit of God is a dove, full of peace and love and kindness, and not a bird of prey. Let me put my hand on that brother's shoulder and say, "Have ye received the Holy Ghost since ye believed?"

Here comes another who breaks into great tempers and fierce anger. The littlest things put him out of temper, and he finds fault. He says that he is very sorry for it afterward, but this does not remove the wounds that he has inflicted. If you cut a person's head off, it is of little use to apologize to him afterward. Many a man boils over with passion and burns his friend and then in cooler moments expresses his regret. All very fine, but fine words cure no blisters. I would suggest they ask this question: "Have I received the Holy Ghost since I believed? Is He not the spirit of peace and gentleness?"

Here is a brother who cannot be happy unless he indulges in worldly amusements. When he gets into a grand frolic with worldly people, he finds himself at home, but the joys of godliness he despises. I should like to meet that brother acting out his worldliness and inquire, "Have ye received the Holy Ghost since ye believed?" You would feel awkward, would you not? Do not do things that make you feel awkward. Keep out of those places that are unfit for a child of God. Though we live in the world, we do not need to play with the devil or his children. Our Lord does not love that His children should make the heirs of wrath their intimates. Such evil communication will bring you misery sooner or later. You cannot expect the Holy Spirit to continue with you if you are joined with the adversaries of the Lord.

There are certain people who live solely to get money, that they may grow rich and grind everybody else to pieces in the process. I would like when the greedy man is adding up his wealth to put to him the question, "Have ye received the Holy Ghost since ye believed?" He would answer, "Don't; it is terribly out of place to mention so serious a matter." It is out of place, no doubt, for the man himself is out of place; but should a believer be in a position where a friend cannot speak to him about his eternal interests?

I know *some to whom the question is needless*. You meet them in the morning, soaring aloft, like a lark, in the praises of God. See them in trouble: they are patient and resigned to their heavenly Father's will. Mark how they spend their lives in service, seeking to win sinners to Christ. Their everyday talk is sweet with the honey of the Holy Land: you cannot be with them ten minutes without discovering that they have leaned upon Jesus' bosom. There is a fragrance about them that tells you that they dwell in the garden of the Lord. When they tell you their experience, it is as if an angel shook his wings. You do not ask them if they have received the Holy Ghost, but you stand still and admire the work of the Spirit of God in them. Now, be such yourselves. If you would be strong and make a lasting impression on others by a living testimony of the truth, you must have the Spirit of God not only in His essential operations but also in His soul-enriching, heart-delighting, life-sanctifying power. Thus will He turn earth into heaven and make us poor, earth-born creatures ready to be partakers of the inheritance of the saints in light.

The Lessons from the Question

First, *we are to look for salvation not to one single act of faith in the past* but to Jesus, in whom we continue to believe. I have read, very much to my grief, that whatever we may be today, we are safe if we exercised a single act of faith in the past. There may be truth in the statement, but it is so badly stated and so wretchedly distorted that it looks like a lie: saving faith does not spend itself in a single act but continues to work and operate throughout the whole of life. It is not a question of believing in the past. The question is, "Do I believe in the Lord Jesus at this hour?" For if my faith is "faith of the operation of God," it has continued to this hour and will continue to the end. All my troubles, temptations, and sins have not killed my faith, but for every day, as the day has come, I have continued to receive the Holy Spirit's gracious aid since I believed. "The just shall live by faith" (Rom. 1:17). It is a principle within, springing up unto everlasting life; it is a living well that never ceases to flow. It is not something I do in five minutes and then am done with it; it is a holy act that I began to do at a certain time but that I shall never cease doing till there remains nothing more to be believed. We must live by faith. It is not only our starting point but also the road along which we are to travel.

The next lesson is that *we must continue to live by receiving.* We received Christ Jesus the Lord at the first, and now we receive the Holy Ghost. The disciples of John were questioned about their receiving rather than their giving, for everything depends upon what we receive. Nothing can come out of us if it does not first go into us. The question is still appropriate, "What hast thou which thou hast not received?" We are always filled out of the fullness of the Lord, for we are not fountains but reservoirs, not creators but receivers. What shall we render unto the Lord for all His benefits toward us? We can only keep on receiving—take the cup of salvation and call upon the name of the Lord.

Again, let us learn that *we may not despise those who are not taught the basics of spiritual life,* not even those who have not so much as heard of the Holy Ghost. Paul did not say, "You are so desperately ignorant that I have no time for you." On the contrary, he sat down and taught them more, and then baptized them. God has some children who are mere babes, and it is a fact for their comfort that He does not judge their being His children by measuring their height. Babes in grace are as much His children as those who have reached perfect adulthood. Those who are weak are dear to God; let them be dear to us. If anyone trusts Christ, God knows enough to take him to heaven and enough for you to take Him into your heart.

Another lesson is that *the Holy Spirit always keeps sweet company with Jesus Christ.* As long as these good people knew only John the Baptist, they might know water baptism, but they could not know the baptism of the Holy Ghost. It was only when they came to know Jesus that the Spirit of God came upon them, and they began to work those mighty things that are the fruits of the Spirit. Learn, then, to keep close to Christ both in your lives and in your teachings. The Spirit of God will not set His seal to what I say or what you say, but He will confirm the testimony of Jesus. The things of God concerning Christ Jesus our Lord shall never be without the attesting power of the Holy Ghost.

Once more, *all believers have more room for the Holy Spirit in their lives.* If anyone has the idea that he cannot have any more grace, I am afraid he is especially in need of it. Perfection is left to the angels. Anyone so good in his own esteem that he cannot be better is cracked in either his head or his honesty. As for you and for me, let us be certain that if we have been taught of the Spirit, there is more light yet for us; if we have been made alive, there is more life for the Spirit to impart; if we have been comforted, there are greater consolations yet; if we have been made strong, we can be stronger yet to do greater exploits; if we have had communion with Christ, we can be closer yet and enter more thoroughly into the secret place of the tabernacle of the Most High. If it can be, why should it not be?

A little religion is a miserable thing. He who has just enough to save him may not have enough to comfort him. He that has much grace and is filled with the Spirit of God shall have two heavens—a heaven here and a heaven hereafter. He who has the Spirit richly shall have the joy of the Lord as his strength and the joy of the Lord hereafter to be his reward. Come, let us ask for all that God is willing to give. Does He not say, "Open thy mouth wide, and I will fill it"? Come, little one, why remain little? Come. You are living on crumbs, why not eat abundantly of the bread of heaven? Do not be content with pennies when a king's ransom is at your disposal. Poor brother, rise out of your poverty. Sister, bowed down by reason of the little of the Spirit of God you have received, believe for more and pray upon a larger scale. May the Lord enlarge your heart and fill it and then enlarge it again and fill it again, so that from day to day we may receive the Holy Ghost, till at the last, Jesus shall receive us into His glory.

The divine communications of the Holy Spirit are the precious heritage of true saints, but they are a peculiar voice to their own souls and are not to be repeated in words. If you know these divine workings, then through His operations you are made to know the Holy Spirit. That deep calm, that peace that only He can give, that exhilaration, that superlative joy as of heaven begun below that only the Lord can work, that steadfast courage, that holy patience, that fixedness of heart, that gentleness of manner and firmness of purpose, which come only from above—these all introduce you to the wonder-working Spirit who takes pleasure to operate upon the minds of the heirs of eternal glory. Thus we know the Holy Spirit by His works and gifts and revelations.

Chapter Eight

An Intimate Knowledge of the Holy Spirit

Even the Spirit of truth; whom the world cannot receive, because it seeth him not, neither knoweth him: but ye know him; for he dwelleth with you, and shall be in you—John 14:17.

THERE IS MUCH MEANING in the expression, "the Spirit of truth." The Spirit of truth is the teacher of truth, pure truth, practical, divinely effective truth. He never teaches anything but the truth. If it comes from the Spirit of God, we may receive it from Him without any hesitation. He takes the things of Christ and shows them to us, thus proving to be the Spirit of truth. He is the very Spirit and soul of truth, the essence, the life, and power of it. Divine truth, when merely heard, makes no effect upon the mind until the Spirit of God gives it life, and then it becomes a quickening force. He makes the truth itself—in its reality and substance—to enter the soul and affect the heart. He is the teacher of truth, the active power that makes the truth to be truth to us in the assurance of our inmost souls.

He is the Spirit of truth in this sense, too—that He works truthfulness in His people. "There is no guile" in those with whom the Holy Ghost works effectually; they are open-minded, honest, sincere, and true; they have an intense affection and passion for the truth. They are by His truthful influence pre-served from deadly error. If it were possible, false teachers would deceive even the elect; but where the Spirit of God dwells, He detects for us the false from the true and gives us the spirit of a sound mind by which we reject that which is false. In this sense, He is the Spirit of truth; and as He works truthfulness in His people, so the work that He does is always true and real work. The Spirit of God works true conversion, sincere repentance, and saving faith, such as no sun of persecution can dry up and wither. He works a deep conviction of sin and simple faith in the Lord Jesus; and these abide in the heart. In the new birth, He imparts a divine life, and the man becomes a child of God. He produces real sanctification—not the pretense of perfection, but the reality of holiness. Everything the Spirit of God does is substance and not shadow. Much of what excites the church is only the work of man, but the eternal, abiding, everlasting work of grace is wrought by the Spirit of truth alone.

We may be sure that whatever He, as the Spirit of truth, sets His seal upon is true. He will bear witness only to truth; He will not assist in maintaining error. Mark this word: the proportion to which the church departs from the truth of God is the degree to which the Spirit of God departs from the church. The Spirit of God can never set His seal to a lie; the testimony of His sacred operation, in "signs following," is borne only to the truth of God. If what I preach is not the Word of the Lord, it will not be fol-lowed by the work of the Spirit of truth; there will be neither conversion nor edification. It is by the truth that the Spirit of God works, and we must be very careful that we do not bring forth any other instrument. Let us never talk as if Scriptural doctrine were of little or no consequence, for where the doctrine is not of God, the Spirit of truth is grieved and will depart from such a ministry. Except we keep close to the words of the Lord Jesus and the revelation of the inspired Book, the Spirit of truth will show His displeasure by refusing to use our words. Your music, your architecture, your learning, and your "bright services" are in vain if the truth is given up. Farewell to the witness of the Spirit in the hearts of men when the inventions of men are taught in the place of the revelation of God.

If the Holy Spirit is bearing witness in your spirit that you are a child of God, you are truly born of God; the presence of the divine Paraclete is the seal of your adoption. If He dwells in you, this is the token of your sonship. If He helps, strengthens, comforts, guides, illuminates, and sanctifies you, you have the seal of God which you need not question.

This is *the* distinction between the men of the world and the disciples of Christ. The world knows nothing of the Holy Spirit; but the disciples of Christ know Him, for the Lord Jesus said, "He dwelleth with you, and shall be in you." There are a great many distinctions in the world of a religious kind, but you cannot judge who the people of God are by external things. Forms of church government and modes of worship may be important in their own place, but the infallible test is this: Do you bear the fruit of the Spirit of God in you? Does He dwell in you? "If any man have not the Spirit of Christ, he is none of his" (Rom. 8:9), but he that has the Spirit dwelling within his soul is a true-born heir of heaven. What a blessed privilege of being on intimate terms with the Holy Ghost: "But ye know him; for he dwelleth with you, and shall be in you."

Believers in Christ Know the Holy Spirit

Believers know the Holy Spirit, to begin with, *by believing what has been taught concerning the Comforter by the Lord Jesus Christ.* When Jesus Christ had taught His people concerning the Holy Spirit and they had received His teaching, He said, "Ye know him; for he dwelleth with you, and shall be in you." If they had refused Christ's words, if they had possessed no love, if they had not kept His commandments, if they had arrogantly resolved to find out this mystery for themselves apart from the instruction of their Master, they would not have known the Spirit of God. We must begin our acquaintance with the Spirit by sitting at the feet of Jesus and accepting His testimony as true.

More than this, however, we know the Holy Spirit *by knowing our Lord Jesus and by His knowing the Father.* There is such an intimate union between the Holy Spirit, the Father, and the Son that to know the Holy Spirit, we must know the Son of God and the Father. If we know the Lord Jesus, we have the Spirit of God, for by no one else could the things of Christ be revealed to us. Beginning, then, at the very beginning, do you know the Lord Jesus Christ? Is He your friend, your acquaintance? Are you on personal terms of fellowship with Him? If so, you see the Father in His face. Jesus said, "He that hath seen me hath seen the Father" (John 14:9), and He tells His people, "From henceforth ye know him, and have seen him" (John 14:7). You are, therefore, acquainted with God the Father through the Son, and you have seen the glory of His grace beaming in your Savior's face. In this way, you have become acquainted with the Holy Spirit, who is not separated from the Father and the Son.

We know the Holy Spirit, next, *by His operations upon us*. Not only do we know about His operations, but we have been the subjects of them. All those who are true disciples of Christ have felt a divinely supernatural power working upon them. First, the Holy Spirit operates to our spiritual quickening. There was a time when we were dead in trespasses and sins: we did not desire, nor did we even know, spiritual things. The Spirit of God came upon us, and we were awakened, aroused, and made alive. Do you remember that? Many of us can distinctly remember when we passed from death to life. With others, the visible life may have been made manifest more gradually, but even in them there was a moment when the vital force entered the soul. In connection with that quickening, there was conviction of sin. In what a powerful light does the Holy Spirit set our sin! When a single beam from the Spirit of truth shines upon sin, it makes it appear "exceeding sinful." I remember Mr. Bunyan's words: "I thought none but the devil himself could equal me for inward wickedness and pollution of mind." When the Spirit of God revealed his heart, he would have willingly changed places with toads and serpents, for he esteemed the most loathsome objects to be better than himself. This revelation of darkness is the effect of light, the light of the Spirit of God; and when He convinces us of sin we begin to know Him.

When, after having convinced us of sin, He leads us to repentance and faith in Jesus Christ, then we know Him! How many promises did you hear, but you could not receive them. Yet when the Spirit of God came, you saw Jesus as the consolation of Israel, the Friend of sinners, the atoning Sacrifice, the

Surety of the covenant of grace; and the sweet peace came streaming into your soul! At that time, you knew not only that the Holy Spirit leads to Jesus Christ but also that He was leading *you*. You knew Him by a personal acquaintance, which is the best of knowledge.

Since that time, we have known the Holy Spirit in many ways: restraining from evil, stimulating to good, instructing, consoling, directing, and enlivening. He has been to us the Spirit of reviving. We have grown dull and cold and sleepy, but no sooner has the Spirit visited us than we have felt all alive. Then our whole heart has run in the ways of God's commands, and we have rejoiced in His name. How true is that word, "He restoreth my soul"! Thus have we known the Holy Spirit by His operations within us.

Many times He has acted as an illuminator. A difficult Scripture has been before me: I have studied the Greek and examined what the finest biblical experts have written upon it; and yet, when I have thus used all the helps within reach, the point has remained in the dark. My best aid has always been to resort to the great Author of the sacred Word, even the Holy Spirit. He can, by blessing the means that we are using or by directly leading our mind in the right track, put an end to all difficulty. He has the clue of every maze, the solution of every riddle; and to whom He wills, He can reveal the secret of the Lord. If you wish to understand the Scriptures, seek this light from above, for this is the true light. Other lights may mislead, but this is clear and sure. To have the Spirit of God lighting up the inner chambers of truth is a great gift. Truth of the deeper sort is comparable to a cavern into which we cannot find our way except by a guide and a light. When the Spirit of truth comes, He pours daylight into the darkness and leads us into all truth. He does not merely show the truth; He leads us into it, so that we stand within it and rejoice in the wondrous treasure that it contains. Then we know Him as our sacred illuminator.

I specially note that we also know Him as the Comforter. Alas for the troubles that we receive in the world. Few things are as we wish, and therefore we are deeply troubled; but when the Spirit of God comes, peace flows to us like a river and Jesus says to us, "Peace be unto you." Do you know that peace? It is possible to know such an inbreaking of the floods of joy that the Holy Spirit creates that death itself not only loses its sting but even becomes a joy. The comforts of the Holy Ghost take bitterness out of wormwood and gall and the sting out of the last enemy. May God help us to know the Holy Spirit as our Comforter! Happy knowledge!

I trust that we have also known the Holy Spirit as guiding us in various ways. I am not saying that any man is inspired as to the future, but I do believe that some believers have received preparations for the future and foreshadowings of their coming experiences. When believers come into difficult circumstances, they bow the knee and cry for guidance, even as David said, "Bring hither the ephod." In some way, not always to be explained, the Spirit of God guides our steps through life if we obey His instructions. Is it not written, "Thine ears shall hear a word behind thee, saying, This is the way, walk ye in it" (Isa. 30:21)? The divine communications of the Holy Spirit are the precious heritage of true saints, but they are a peculiar voice to their own souls and are not to be repeated in words. If you know these divine workings, then through His operations you are made to know the Holy Spirit. That deep calm, that peace that only He can give, that exhilaration, that superlative joy as of heaven begun below that only the Lord can work, that steadfast courage, that holy patience, that fixedness of heart, that gentleness of manner and firmness of purpose, which come only from above—these all introduce you to the wonder-working Spirit who takes pleasure to operate upon the minds of the heirs of eternal glory. Thus we know the Holy Spirit by His works and gifts and revelations.

I do not think we have entered the center of the text even yet. "Ye know *Him*"—*not only His works, but Himself.* I may know an artist's paintings, but I may not know the artist. "Ye know him," says our Lord; and truly we know the Holy Ghost as to His personality. If the Holy Ghost were a mere influence, we should read, "Ye know *it*." Let us always shun the mistake of calling the Holy Ghost "*it*." *It* is a dead thing: the Holy Ghost is a living, blessed person, and I hope we can say that we know Him as such. Others may doubt His personality, but we believe the teaching of our Lord Jesus Christ and behold—in the names given to Him, the emotions ascribed to Him, and the acts performed by Him—abundant proofs of His sacred personality. In our hearts we know *Him*.

As we know His personality, so we know also His divinity, because the Holy Ghost works in us effects that none but God could work. Who can give life to the spiritually dead? Who can instruct and illuminate as the Holy Spirit does? Only because He is divine can He guide us into all truth and purify us unto perfect holiness. There have been things wrought in us, in our experience, in which we have beheld not only the finger of God but also God Himself working in our hearts to will and to do of His own good pleasure. Oh, worship the Holy Spirit! The greatest crime of sinners is to blaspheme the Holy Ghost, and the greatest fault of saints is to neglect the Holy Ghost. Let us adore Him, yield to Him, confide in Him, and pray that we may know Him to the full.

So it comes to this—that as we know the Holy Spirit's personality and Godhead, we have come to know *Him*. I mean this—that there is now a personal relationship between the believer and the Holy Ghost, a conscious fellowship and communion. Do we not enjoy it? We speak with Him, and He speaks with us. We trust Him, and He entrusts us with many a precious truth. We are not strangers now. We do not talk of Him as a distant person of whom we have heard, a divine mystery with which prophets and apostles were acquainted in remote ages; but we know Him. Let me ask you, Is this true or not? If you are obliged to say, "I do not know whether there is any Holy Ghost," then I pray the Lord to deal graciously with you and manifest His Son Jesus Christ to you by the power of the same Holy Spirit of whom we speak. The Spirit of truth is more familiar with us than any other person, for He enters within, where none else find admission.

Believers Know the Holy Spirit Through Himself

Read the text again: "Ye know him; for he dwelleth with you, and shall be in you." It is not ". . . for ye have heard gracious preaching" or ". . . for ye have read about him in the Scriptures."

As the moon cannot help us see the sun, so a man cannot reveal God. God can only be seen in His own light. No one can reveal the Holy Spirit but the Holy Spirit. Why is that?

I answer, first, because of *the inadequacy of all means.* By what methods can you make a man know the Holy Ghost? He is not to be discerned by the senses or perceived by eyes or ears. What if the preacher is eloquent as an angel. In what way would that make you know the Holy Ghost? You would probably remember more of the man than of his subject. Nothing is more to be deplored than a hungering after mere oratory. It would be infinitely better to speak stammeringly the truth than to pour forth a flood of words in which the truth is drowned. Words are nothing but air and wind, and they cannot possibly reveal the Holy Spirit.

No church ordinance or symbol can express the Holy Spirit. If He were even to descend upon us as a dove, we should see the visible shape but not necessarily discern the Spirit. The Spirit Himself must reveal Himself. There is no chariot in which God can ride to us: the axles of creation itself would break beneath the enormous load of Deity. It is not possible for God to reveal Himself fully by His works: He is seen only by Himself. Hence the Son of God has come to us as "God with us." In Him we see God. The Holy Spirit must come into the heart to which He would make Himself known.

This is even more clear from *the inability of our nature to discover the Holy Spirit.* We are spiritually dead: how can we know anything until He makes us alive? Our eyes are spiritually blind: how can we see Him until He opens our eyes? We are altogether without strength: how can we run after Him until He first comes to us and gives us the power to do so? We are unable to perceive the Holy Spirit, for "the natural man receiveth not the things of the Spirit of God . . . neither can he know them, because they are spiritually discerned" (1 Cor. 2:14). Flesh cannot transform itself into spirit. It is the Lord Himself who must come and breathe into us the Spirit of life, and then we perceive Him who is the Spirit of truth.

Another proof is gathered *from the nature of the case.* The only way to know a man is to meet him and speak to him. You cannot even accurately judge a man by his writings. Actually, you must live with the man to know him. You must live with the Holy

Spirit and He must dwell with you and be in you before you can speak of knowing Him at all.

The facts of the case prove this. Have you not found it so in your own case? Recall when you heard a powerful sermon but walked away feeling lifeless and unmoved. Have you not said to yourself, "I am as hard as stone and as cold as a winter's fog? What shall I do?" Thus are you without the Spirit of God; but when the divine Spirit comes upon you, such complaints end. Then does the lame man leap and the tongue of the dumb is made to sing. Then are you full of living joy in listening to the gospel. Every word you hear seems to be on wheels, and toward you the cherubim fly swiftly bringing live coals from the altar.

Believers Enjoy a Sacred Intimacy with the Spirit of God

First, he says, *"he dwelleth with you."* Is that not a wonderful sentence? The Holy Ghost is God, and therefore the heaven of heavens cannot contain Him, and yet behold the condescending fact: "he dwelleth with you." The Holy Spirit is now upon earth, the representative of the Lord Jesus Christ, who said, "I will send you another Comforter"—that is, another Helper and Advocate like Himself. Consider how our Lord lived with His disciples, for in the same way the Spirit of truth dwells with us. Jesus permitted His disciples the most intimate relationship with Himself: they ran to Him with their troubles, their difficulties, their doubts. He was their Master and Lord, and yet He washed their feet. He ate and drank with them. You never find our Lord repelling their approaches or resenting their familiarities. He did not draw a circle around Himself and say, "Keep your distance." In the same manner the Spirit of truth deals with believers. "He dwelleth with you." You may go to Him at any time; you may ask what you will of Him; you may speak to Him as a man speaks with his friend. You cannot see Him, but He sees you, which is much better. You cannot hear His voice, but He hears your voice. He hears your thoughts without a voice.

Dwelling with us, He fulfills the promise of our Lord, "Lo, I am with you always, *even* unto the end of the world" (Matt.

28:20). It is by the Holy Spirit that the Lord Jesus is with us: that we might enjoy that sacred presence, it was expedient for our Lord to go away. What a mercy it is when the Holy Ghost meets with us when we gather! What a dreary business it is when the Holy Ghost is gone from the congregation! The people come and go, and perhaps there may be fine music, admirable eloquence, a vast crowd, or a wealthy congregation. But what of these things? They are a bag of wind! If the Holy Spirit is not in the congregation, it is gathered together in vain.

The Holy Spirit also comes into our homes: "he dwelleth with you." Where do you live? Is it a poor lodging? "He dwelleth with you." It may be you live on board ship and are tossed by the sea, but "he dwelleth with you." Perhaps you go to work in a mine, far beneath the surface of the earth, still, "he dwelleth with you." Many saints are bedridden, but the Spirit dwells with them. I commend this gracious promise to anyone who loves the Lord. The first disciples said to the Lord Jesus, "Master, where dwellest thou?" He answered, "Come and see." So do I bid you to note where the divine Spirit chooses to dwell. Behold and wonder: He dwells with His people wherever they are. He does not leave them alone, but He abides with them as a shepherd with His flock.

Well may we know Him, for He takes up His abode with us and works in the place where He dwells. He makes our members instruments of His working and sanctifies the faculties of our nature as vessels of a temple wherein He dwells. He perfumes every chamber of the house and consecrates every corner of our being. "He dwelleth with you" in all the might of His Godhead, and you are made strong in the inner man by His strengthening. Fall back upon the Holy Ghost in the moment of your weakness. Fall back upon the Holy Spirit at all times. Even in the prayer in which you seek strength, ask that the Spirit may help your weaknesses. Even for the faith that brings you all grace, ask for the Spirit of God to work faith in you. "He dwelleth with you," for you are unable to live without His constant presence, and you need not attempt the perilous experiment.

The second sentence runs, *"he shall be in you."* This is a greater marvel. "Know ye not that your body is the temple of the Holy Ghost?" (1 Cor. 6:19). Take care of them; never defile them. Let no sin come near you; for it is written, "If any man defile the temple of God, him shall God destroy" (1 Cor. 3:17). With what reverence should we look upon the body now that it has been redeemed by the Lord Jesus and is indwelt by the Holy Spirit? The Spirit also dwells within your mind. We possess Him, and He possesses us. "He shall be in you," as a king in his palace or a soul in its body.

The Spirit of God is in you—in your mind, your heart, your desires, your fears, your hopes, your inmost life. The Spirit must permeate your entire being, filling it full with His floods, even as the waters cover the channels of the deep. "He shall be in you." It is a wonderful fact, but believers realize it. The Spirit shall be in you as the source and the force of your life. What cannot a man do when the Holy Spirit is in him? His weakest endeavor will prosper when the Holy Spirit is pouring His life into him. But without the Holy Spirit, what barren and withered trees we are! May we never know the awful drought that comes of the absence of the Spirit!

When our Lord Jesus Christ came upon the earth, that was to us *the pledge* of the indwelling of the Holy Ghost in us: for as God dwelt in the human person of the Lord Jesus Christ, even so the Spirit abides in our humanity. Our Lord's life on earth was *the picture* of the Spirit's indwelling. As He was anointed of the Spirit, even so are we in our measure. "Jesus Christ . . . went about doing good" (Acts 10:38). He lived consecrated to God, loving the sons of men. Thus will the Spirit of God within us cause us to live: we shall imitate the Christ of God through the Spirit of God.

The death of Christ was *the way* by which the Spirit was enabled to come to sinful men. By His great sacrifice, the stone is rolled away that once blocked the road. When our Lord rose from the dead, we had *the guarantee* that even so the Spirit of God would quicken our mortal bodies and renew us into newness of life. But it was when our Lord ascended, leading captivity captive, that the Holy Spirit was *to the full, actually given*. When our Redeemer returned to His father's throne, He scattered the treasures of heaven: He gave the Holy Spirit to men of various offices and to His whole church; then were the days of refreshing by divine visitation. Your ascended Lord gives you this token of

His love—the indwelling of the Holy Ghost in you: prize it above all things. Do you know it? I have urged the question upon myself, and therefore I urge it upon you. Does the Spirit of truth dwell in you? If not, what will you do?

Believers Shall Experience an Increase of the Spirit's Intimacy

"He dwelleth with you, and shall be in you." Mark well the increase. Is it not a blessed step from *with* to *in*? *With* is a friend in the same house; *in* is a spirit within yourself. This is nearer, dearer, more mysterious and effective by far. What a distinct advance it is for the child of God when he rises from the Spirit of God being *with* him to being *in* him! When the Spirit of God helped the apostles to work miracles, He was *with* them; but when they came to feel His spiritual work in their souls and to rejoice in the comfort that He brought to them, then He was *in* them. Even if you could obtain miraculous gifts, you ought not to be satisfied to speak with tongues or to work miracles, but you should press on to know the Spirit within—indwelling, communing, quickening you.

"He shall be in you." Notice that in consequence of this, we know Him. If a person dwells with us, we begin to know him. But if he dwells within us, becoming intertwined with our being, then we know Him indeed. This is a high degree of intimacy.

As we have noticed the increase, so mark the continuance: "he *shall be* in you." There is no period in which the Holy Spirit will have finished His work so as to go away and leave the believer to Himself. Our Savior says of the Comforter that He "shall abide with you forever." Grieve not the Spirit of God, quench Him not, resist Him not; but carefully cherish in your hearts this divine word: "he shall be in you." What comfort is here! You dread the days of old age and infirmity, but "he shall be in you." You tremble before that trial that threatens you, but "he shall be in you." And when the last moment approaches, when you must breathe out your soul to God, the living Spirit who dwells with you shall then be *in* you, and by His living power within shall transform death into the gate of endless life. Child of God, your

Comforter will not leave you. He will continue still to take up His residence within you until you shall be taken up to dwell where Jesus is forever and ever.

This is our great reliance for the future upholding of the church as a whole and of each individual believer: the Spirit of God dwells with us and shall be in us. The church of God will never be destroyed. The gates of hell shall not prevail against her, for the Holy Ghost dwells with us and shall be in us to the end of the world. This is the reliance of the child of God personally for His perseverance in grace. He knows that Jesus lives, and therefore he shall live, and the Holy Spirit is within him as the life of Christ, which can never die. The believer pushes on, despite a thousand obstacles, knowing that God gives him the victory through the Lord Jesus Christ, out of whose hand none can pluck him.

If you have never known the Spirit of God, may you feel His power coming upon you at this moment! The other day, the ground was hard as iron, and the water was turned to ice; but there came a breath from the south and soon a thaw set in, the snow vanished, and the ice was gone. Even so the Holy Spirit breathes on us, and our inward frost disappears at once. Come, Holy Spirit. Come even now.

If we obtain an audience with a king, we do not cry; we speak in measured tones and set phrases. But the Spirit of God takes away the formality, leading us to cry. When we cry, we cry "Abba." Even our very cries are full of the spirit of adoption. And what child minds his father hearing him cry? When the Spirit in us sends forth cries and groans, we are not ashamed, nor are we afraid to cry before God. I know some of you think that God will not hear your prayers because you cannot pray grandly like such-and-such a person. Oh, but the Spirit of His Son cries, and you cannot do better than cry, too. Be satisfied to offer to God broken language, words salted with your griefs, wetted with your tears. Go to Him with holy familiarity and be not afraid to cry in His presence, "Abba, Father."

Chapter Nine

Adoption—the Spirit and the Cry

And because ye are sons, God hath sent forth the Spirit of his Son into your hearts, crying, Abba, Father—Galatians 4:6.

ALTHOUGH WE DO NOT FIND the doctrine of the Trinity in Unity set forth in Scripture in the formal terms of the Athanasian creed, the truth is continually taken for granted. In many passages it is so prominently displayed that it requires willful blindness to not see it. In the present verse, for instance, we have distinct mention of each of the three divine Persons. "God," that is, the Father, "sent forth the Spirit," that is, the Holy Spirit; and He is here called "the Spirit *of His Son.*" There is the mention not only of the separate names but also of specific operations to each. It is plain that you have here the distinct personality of each. Neither the Father, the Son, nor the Spirit can be an influence or a mere form of existence, for each acts in a divine manner but with a special sphere and a distinct mode of operation. When, for instance, the Holy Ghost is said to be "crying, Abba, Father," we understand that an influence cannot cry; the act requires a person to perform it. Though we may not comprehend the wonderful truth of the undivided Unity and the distinct personality of the Triune Godhead, yet, nevertheless, we see the truth revealed in the Holy Scriptures; therefore, we accept it as a matter of faith.

Within the compass of this one verse, believers are made to see how needful is the cooperation of the entire Trinity to our salvation, and they are charmed to see the loving union of all in the work of deliverance. We reverence the Father, without whom we had not been chosen or adopted: the Father who "hath begotten us again unto a lively hope by the resurrection of Jesus Christ from the dead" (1 Pet. 1:3). We love and reverence the Son, by whose most precious blood we have been redeemed and with whom we are one in a mystic and everlasting union. And we adore and love the divine Spirit, for it is by Him that we have been regenerated, illuminated, quickened, preserved, and sanctified; and it is through Him that we receive the seal and witness within our hearts, by which we are assured that we are indeed the sons of God. We must not fail to bless, adore, and love each one of the exalted Persons, but we must diligently bow in lowliest reverence before the one God—Father, Son, and Holy Ghost.

With the wonder of the Trinity as our backdrop, let us come to the text itself and consider the specific marvel of our adoption into the family of God. Three things are clearly set forth: the first is the *dignity of the believers*—"ye are sons"; the second is *the consequent indwelling of the Holy Ghost*—"because ye are sons, God hath sent forth the Spirit of His Son into your hearts"; and the third is *the cry of sonship*—crying, "Abba, Father."

The Dignity of Believers

Adoption gives us the rights of children; regeneration gives us the nature of children: we are partakers of both of these, for we are children of God.

Let us here observe that *this sonship is a gift of grace received by faith*. The Jews claimed to be of the family of God, but their privileges came to them by way of their physical birth. We have a sonship that does not come to us by nature, for we are "born, not of blood, nor of the will of the flesh, nor of the will of man, but of God" (John 1:13). Our sonship comes by promise, by the operation of God as a special gift to a people set apart to the Lord by His own sovereign grace, as Isaac was. This honor and privilege come to us, according to the connection of our text, by faith. Note well the twenty-sixth verse of the preceding chapter: "For ye are all the children of God by faith in Christ Jesus" (Gal. 3:26). As unbelievers we know nothing of adoption. While we are under the law as self-righteous we know something of servitude, but we know nothing of sonship. It is only after that faith has come that we cease to be under the schoolmaster and rise out of minority to take the privileges of the sons of God.

Faith works in us the spirit of adoption and our consciousness of sonship in this manner: first, *it brings us justification*. Verse twenty-four of chapter three says, "Wherefore the law was our schoolmaster *to bring us* unto Christ, that we might be justified by faith." An unjustified man stands in the condition of a criminal, not of a child: his sin is laid to his charge; he is reckoned as unjust and unrighteous, a rebel against his king, and not a child enjoying his father's love. But when faith realizes the cleansing power of the blood of atonement and claims the righteousness of God in Christ Jesus, the justified man becomes a son and a child. Justification and adoption always go together.

Faith brings us into the realization of our adoption in the next place by *setting us free from the bondage of the law*. "But after that faith is come, we are no longer under a schoolmaster" (Gal. 3:25). When we groaned under a sense of sin and were shut up by it as in a prison, our best attempts to keep the law brought us into yet another bondage, which became harder and harder as failure succeeded to failure. We sinned and stumbled more and more to our soul's confusion. But now that faith has come, we see the law fulfilled in Christ and ourselves justified and accepted in Him. This changes the slave into a child and duty into choice. Now we delight in the law; and by the power of the Spirit, we walk in holiness to the glory of God. Thus it is that by believing in Christ Jesus we escape from Moses, the taskmaster, and come to Jesus, the Savior. We cease to regard God as an angry Judge and view Him as our loving Father. The rule of grace, gratitude, and love prevails and is one of the grand privileges of the children of God.

Now, *faith is the mark of sonship in all who have it*, whoever they are, for "ye are all the children of God by faith in Christ Jesus" (Gal. 3:26). If you are believing in Jesus, whether you are Jew or Gentile, bond or free, you are a son of God. Sonship belongs to him who has the smallest degree of faith and is no more than a babe in grace. When a man believes in Jesus Christ, his name is in the register book of the great family above. But if you have no faith, no matter what zeal, works, knowledge, or pretensions to holiness you may possess, you are nothing, and your religion is in vain. Without faith in Christ you are as sounding brass and a tinkling cymbal, for without faith it is impossible to please God.

This according to the apostle is further illustrated by our baptism, for in baptism, if there is faith in the soul, there is an open putting on of the Lord Jesus Christ. Read the next verse: "For as many of you as have been baptized into Christ have put on Christ" (Gal. 3:27). In baptism you professed to be dead to the world, and you were therefore buried into the name of Jesus; dead to everything but Christ, and henceforth your life was to be in Him, and you were to be as one raised from the dead to newness of life. The spirit and essence of the ordinance lie in the soul's entering into the symbol, in the man's knowing not only the baptism into water but also the baptism into the Holy Ghost and into fire. As many as know that inward mystic baptism into Christ know also they have put on Christ and are covered by Him as a man is by his garment. Henceforth you are one in Christ, you bear His name, you live in Him, you are altogether His. Now, if you are one with Christ, since He is a Son, you are sons also. That which belongs to Christ also belongs to you. As the Roman youth when he came of age put on the *toga* and was admitted to the rights of citizenship, so the putting on of Christ is the token of our admission into the position and enjoyment of our glorious heritage as sons of God.

Adoption comes to us by redemption. Read the passage that precedes the text: "But when the fulness of time was come, God sent forth his Son, made of a woman, made under the law, to redeem them that were under the law, that we might receive the adoption of sons" (Gal. 4:4–5). Prize redemption and never listen to any teaching that would destroy its meaning or lower its importance. Remember that you were redeemed not with silver and gold but with the precious blood of Christ. You were under the law and subject to its curse, for you had broken it most grievously. You were also under the terror of the law, for you feared its wrath. But now you are redeemed, and this because Christ came under the law and kept it by both His active and His passive obedience, fulfilling all its commands and bearing all its penalty on your behalf and in your place. Henceforth you are the redeemed of the Lord and enjoy a liberty that comes by no other way than that of eternal ransom. Glory be to our redeeming Lord, by whom we have received the adoption!

We further learn from the passage that *we now enjoy the privilege of sonship.* The apostle means not only that we are children but also that we are full-grown children. "Because ye are sons" means that—in contrast to the Old Testament believers—the time appointed by the Father has come and believers in Christ are of legal age and no longer under tutors and governors. Till faith in Christ comes, we are under guardians, like mere boys or minors; but after faith, we take our rights as sons of God. The Jewish church of old was under the yoke of the law. Its sacrifices were continual and its ceremonies endless; new moons and feasts must be kept; jubilees must be observed and pilgrimages made. In fact, the yoke was too heavy for feeble flesh to bear. The law followed the Israelite into every corner and dealt with him upon every point. It treated him like a boy at school that has a rule for everything. Now that faith has come we are full-grown sons, and therefore we are free from the rules that govern the school of the child. We are under law to Christ—a law of love and not of fear, of grace and not of bondage. This is the liberty of the children of God.

Now, by faith *we are no more bond servants.* The apostle says that "the heir, as long as he is a child, differeth nothing from a servant, though he be lord of all" (Gal. 4:1). But he adds that we are now the sons of God and have come of age: we are free to enjoy the honors and blessings of the Father's house. Rejoice that the free spirit dwells within you and prompts you to holiness. This is a far superior power to the bondage to outward forms and rites and ceremonies. The Spirit of God teaches you all things and leads you into the inner meaning and substance of the truth.

Now, also, says the apostle, *we are heirs*—"Wherefore thou art no more a servant, but a son; and if a son, then an heir of God through Christ" (Gal. 4:7). No living man has ever realized to the full extent what this means. Believers are at this moment heirs, but what is the estate? It is God Himself! We are heirs of God! Not only heirs of the promises and blessings of His Word, but heirs of God Himself. David said, "The LORD is the portion of mine inheritance and of my cup" (Ps. 16:5). As God said to Abraham, "Fear not, Abram: I *am* thy shield, *and* thine exceeding great reward" (Gen. 15:1), so He says to every man who is born of the Spirit. Why, then, O believer, are you poor? All riches are yours. Why, then, are you sorrowful? The ever-blessed God is yours. Why do you tremble? Omnipotence waits to help you. Why do you distrust? His faithfulness will abide with you even to the end. All things are yours, for Christ is yours and Christ is God's. We enjoy even now the pledge and earnest of heaven in the indwelling of the Holy Ghost. Oh, what privileges belong to those who are the sons of God!

Once more upon this point of the believer's dignity, *we are already tasting one of the inevitable consequences of being the sons of God*. What are they? One of them is opposition. No sooner had the Apostle Paul preached the liberty of the saints than immediately there arose certain teachers who said, "This will never do: you must be circumcised, you must come under the law." Their opposition was an evidence to Paul of the truth they had experienced. You shall find that if you enjoy fellowship with God, if you live in the spirit of adoption, those who are under bondage to the law will quarrel with you. As the apostle says, "As then he that was born after the flesh persecuted him that was born after the Spirit, even so it is now" (Gal. 4:29).

There have been periods in which the enemies of the true gospel have imprisoned and burned alive the lovers of the gospel. At present, mockings are still to be endured, our words are twisted, our intentions are misrepresented, and all sorts of horrible things are attributed to us. Do not be surprised when this happens to you, but let it be a confirmation of your faith in Christ Jesus, for He said, "If ye were of the world, the world would love his own: but because ye are not of the world, but I have chosen you out of the world, therefore the world hateth you" (John 15:19).

The Indwelling of the Holy Ghost

"God hath sent forth the Spirit of his Son into your hearts." *Here is a divine act of the Father*. The Holy Ghost proceeds from the Father and the Son, and God has sent Him into your hearts. When Jehovah sent Him to your heart, He made His way without violating your will, but yet with irresistible power. Where Jehovah sent Him, there He will abide. As surely as God sent His Son into the world to dwell among men so that His saints beheld His glory, so surely God sent the Spirit to enter men's hearts, there to dwell that the glory of God may also be revealed.

Note the style and title under which the Holy Spirit comes to us: *He comes as the Spirit of Jesus.* The words are "the Spirit of his Son," not meaning the character and disposition of Christ, though that were quite true, but it means the Holy Ghost. Why, then, is He called the Spirit of His Son or the Spirit of Jesus? May we not give these reasons? It was by the Holy Ghost that the human nature of Christ was born of the virgin. By the Spirit our Lord was attested at His baptism when the Holy Spirit descended upon Him like a dove. In Him the Holy Spirit dwelt without measure, anointing Him for His great work. The Spirit was also with Him, attesting His ministry by signs and wonders. The Holy Ghost is our Lord's great gift to the church; it was after His ascension that He bestowed the gifts of Pentecost and the Holy Spirit descended upon the church to abide with the people of God forever. For these and many other reasons He is called "the Spirit of his Son," and it is He who comes to dwell in believers. I urge you very solemnly and gratefully to consider the wondrous condescension that is here displayed. God the Holy Ghost takes up his residence in believers. Year after year, century after century, He still abides in the saints, and will do so till the elect are all in glory.

Now notice *the place where He takes up His residence*—"God hath sent forth the Spirit of his Son *into your hearts.*" Note that he does not say into your heads or your brains. The Spirit of God doubtless illuminates the intellect and guides the judgment, but this is not the main part of His work. He comes to dwell in the heart, for with the heart man believes unto righteousness. The heart is the center of our being, and therefore the Holy Ghost comes into the central fortress and universal citadel of our nature, taking possession of the whole. It is from the heart and through the heart that life is diffused. When the Spirit of God takes possession of the heart, He operates upon every power and faculty and member of our entire being. Out of the heart are the issues of life, and from the affections sanctified by the Holy Ghost, all other faculties and powers receive renewal, illumination, sanctification, strengthening, and ultimate perfection.

This wonderful blessing is ours "because we are sons," and *it is filled with marvelous results*. Sonship sealed by the indwelling Spirit brings us peace and joy. It leads to nearness to God and fellowship with Him. It excites trust, love, and holy passion and creates in us reverence, obedience, and actual likeness to God. All this and much more because the Holy Ghost has come to dwell in us. Oh, matchless mystery! Had it not been revealed, it would never have been imagined; and now that it is revealed, it would never have been believed if it had not actually been experienced by those who are in Christ.

The Cry of Sonship

Where the Holy Ghost enters there is a cry. "God hath sent forth the Spirit of his Son, crying, 'Abba, Father.' " Notice, *it is the Spirit of God that cries*—a most remarkable fact. The apostle in Romans 8:15 says, "ye have received the Spirit of adoption, whereby *we* cry, Abba, Father," but here he describes the Spirit Himself as crying "Abba, Father." We are certain that when he ascribed the cry of "Abba, Father" to us, he did not exclude the Spirit's cry, because in Romans 8:26 he says, "Likewise . . . the Spirit itself maketh intercession for us with groanings which cannot be uttered." Thus He represents the Spirit Himself as groaning with unutterable groanings within the child of God, so that when he wrote to the Romans, he had on his mind the same thought that he expressed to the Galatians. How is this? Is it not ourselves that cry? Yes, assuredly, and yet the Spirit cries also. The expressions are both correct. The Holy Spirit prompts and inspires the cry. He puts the cry into the heart and mouth of the believer. It is His cry because He suggests it, approves of it, and educates us to it. As a mother teaches her child to speak, so He puts this cry of "Abba, Father" into our mouths; yea, it is He who forms in our hearts the desire after our Father God and keeps it there. He is the Spirit of adoption and the Author of adoption's special and significant cry.

Not only does He prompt us to cry, but He works in us a sense of need that compels us to cry and also that spirit of confidence that emboldens us to claim such a relationship to the great God. Nor is this all, for He assists us in some mysterious manner so that we are able to pray correctly. He puts His divine energy into us so that we cry "Abba, Father" in an acceptable manner. There are times when *we* cannot cry at all, and then He cries in us. There are seasons when doubt and fears abound and so choke us that we cannot even raise a cry. Then the indwelling Spirit makes intercession for us, crying in our name according to the will of God. Thus does the cry "Abba, Father" rise up in our hearts even when we feel we could not pray. On the other hand, at times our soul gives such a sweet assent to the Spirit's cry that it becomes ours also, but then we more than ever own the work of the Spirit and still ascribe to Him the blessed cry, "Abba, Father."

I want you to notice a very sweet fact about this cry—namely, that *it is literally the cry of the Son.* God has sent the Spirit of His Son into our hearts, and that Spirit cries in us exactly according to the cry of the Son. If you turn to Mark 14:36, it records that our Lord prayed in the garden, "Abba, Father, all things *are* possible unto thee; take away this cup from me: nevertheless not what I will, but what thou wilt." So this cry in us copies the cry of our Lord to the letter: "Abba, Father." The first word is Aramaic or, roughly speaking, *Abba* is the Hebrew word for "father." The second word is in Greek and is the Gentile word that also signifies father. It is said that these two words are used to remind us that Jews and Gentiles are one before God. The words do remind us of this, but this cannot have been the principal reason for their use. Do you think that when our Lord was in His agony in the garden that He said, "Abba, Father," because Jews and Gentiles are one? It seems to me that our Lord said "Abba" because it was His native tongue. When a Frenchman prays, if he has learned English, he may ordinarily pray in English, but if ever he falls into an agony, he will pray in French, as surely as he prays at all. Our Lord in His agony used His native language, and as born of the seed of Abraham, He cries in his own tongue, "Abba." Even so, we are prompted by the spirit of adoption to use our own language, the language of the heart, and so to speak to the Lord freely in our own tongue.

To my mind, the word *Abba* is of all words in all languages the most natural word for father. It is truly a child's word; and our Master felt, I have no doubt, in His agony, a love for child's words. I think this sweet word *Abba* was chosen to show us that we are to be very natural with God and not stilted and formal. We are to be very affectionate, to come close to Him and be bold to lie in His bosom, looking up into His face and speaking with holy boldness. "Abba" is not a word, somehow, but a babe's lisping. Oh how near we are to God when we can use such speech! How dear He is to us and dear we are to Him when we may thus address Him, saying, like the great Son Himself, "Abba, Father."

This leads me to observe that *this cry in our hearts is exceedingly near and familiar*. Not only is it childlike, but the tone and manner of utterance are equally so. Note that it is *a cry*. If we obtain an audience with a king, we do not cry; we speak in measured tones and set phrases. But the Spirit of God takes away the formality, leading us to *cry*. When we cry, we cry "Abba." Even our very cries are full of the spirit of adoption. And what child minds his father hearing him cry? When the Spirit in us sends forth cries and groans, we are not ashamed, nor are we afraid to cry before God. I know some of you think that God will not hear your prayers because you cannot pray grandly like such-and-such a person. Oh, but the Spirit of His Son cries, and you cannot do better than cry, too. Be satisfied to offer to God broken language, words salted with your griefs, wetted with your tears. Go to Him with holy familiarity and be not afraid to cry in His presence, "Abba, Father."

But then *how fervent it is*, for a cry is an intense thing. A cry is not a flippant utterance but is something that comes up from the soul. Has not the Lord taught us to cry to Him in prayer with fervent importunity that will not take a denial? Has He not brought us so near to Him that sometimes we say, "I will not let You go except You bless me"? We cry after Him, our heart and our flesh cry out for God, for the living God, and this is the cry: "Abba, Father, I must know You, I must taste Your love, I must dwell under Your wing, I must behold Your face, I must feel Your great fatherly heart overflowing and filling my heart with peace." We cry, "Abba, Father."

Finally, I notice that *the most of this crying is kept within the heart* and does not come out verbally. Like Moses, we cry without speaking. God has sent forth the Spirit of His Son *into our hearts*, whereby we cry, "Abba, Father." You know what I mean: it is not only in private prayer that you cry to God, but you call Him "Abba, Father" as you go about the streets or in the workplace. The Spirit of His Son is crying, "Abba, Father" when you are in the crowd or at your table among the family. The Spirit of God makes you cry "Abba, Father," but the cry is mainly in your heart; and there it is so commonly uttered that it becomes the habit of your soul to be crying to your heavenly Father.

The text does not say that He had cried, but the expression is *"crying"*—it is a present participle, indicating that He cries every day. Wake up in the morning and let your first thought be "My Father, my Father, be with me today." Go out into business, and when things perplex you, let that be your refuge: "My Father, help me in this hour of need." When you go home and meet with family worries, let your cry still be, "Help me, my Father." When alone you are not alone, because the Father is with you; and in the midst of the crowd, you are not in danger, because the Father Himself loves you.

What a blessed word: "The Father Himself loves you"! Go and live as His child. Take heed that you reverence Him, for if He is a Father, where is His fear? Go and obey Him, for this is right. Be imitators of God as dear children. Honor Him wherever you are by adorning His doctrine in all things. Go and live upon Him, for you shall soon live with Him. Go and rejoice in Him. Go and cast all your cares upon Him. And whatever men may see in your life, may they be compelled to say that you are a child of the Highest.

When the Spirit of God comes into a man with power so as to fill his soul, He brings to the man's soul a joy, a delight, an elevation of mind, a delightful and healthy excitement that lift him up above the dull dead-level of ordinary life and cause him to rejoice with joy unspeakable and full of glory. I commend this exhilaration to you. It is safe delight because it is holy delight; holy delight because it is the Holy Spirit that works in you, and He makes you to delight in everything that is pleasing to the Holy God. One no longer needs to seek another source of excitement, for here is something more safe, more suitable, more sacred, more ennobling: "Be filled with the Spirit."

Chapter Ten

Be Filled with the Spirit

And be not drunk with wine, wherein is excess; but be filled with the Spirit—Ephesians 5:18.

READING THE FOURTH AND FIFTH chapters of Paul's letter to the Ephesian believers, one needs to realize the elevation and the purity of the apostle's teachings as they must have appeared to the inhabitants of such a wicked city as Ephesus. When first read, these precepts must have seemed like an unearthly light. Today we take for granted a public opinion that condemns drunkenness, lying, and many other vices, which were scarcely considered wrong by that degraded people. Christianity had not affected public sentiment at the time, a sentiment that was distinctly immoral. The sin of fornication was hardly considered sinful; theft was common; lying was universal and was wrong only if you were caught.

Drunkenness, although not regarded as commendable, was looked upon as a failing of great minds but did not come under condemnation. Alexander the Great died through drink. He offered a prize on one occasion to those who could drink the most, and in that famous drinking bout, large numbers of his chieftains and nobility died in the attempt to rival others. Even a man like Socrates was said to be famous for the amount he could drink.

The stories of the feasts of that age I would be ashamed to repeat. Drunkenness, gluttony, and the like were common faults both of the great and of the small, for while poverty kept some from an opportunity for gluttony, men failed to be gluttons only for that reason and not from principle.

The apostle sets before his new converts not a modified system of right and wrong but the purest virtues and the most heavenly graces. As the ages have rolled on, we have seen the wisdom of holding up from the beginning an elevated standard both of doctrine and of practice. We must not bring the standard down to people, but bring people up to the standard. We may not, with the design of making converts more rapidly, alter the pure Word with which our Lord has entrusted us.

My purpose, though, is not to deal with the sin of drunkenness, although I have much to say against it. Of all sins in our country today, drunkenness brings the most present misery upon mankind. Other sins may seem to go deeper into the soul and are more subject to legal punishment, but for creating widespread suffering upon the innocent, upon the wife, and upon the child, this vice raises its head above all others. It throngs our prisons, fills our jails, crowds our mental institutions, and fills our cemeteries with bodies of men and women who die before their time. It is the Moloch of the nineteenth century.

In this passage, the apostle was guided by the Holy Spirit to put in apposition and, in some respects, in opposition, a prohibition and a command: "*Be not drunk with wine, wherein is excess, but be filled with the Spirit.*" Paul had a reason for putting these two things together. There is a very wide and deep abyss between being drunk with wine and being filled with the Spirit. Drunkenness is down, down, down to the depths of the brute, and far lower still; fullness with the Spirit is up, up, up to the very heights of God. However did it happen, then, that in the same verse Paul should put the two together—the prohibition and the command? There were two very good reasons. The first is that *there is a parallel between them*—a degree of similarity despite their infinite difference. Second, he so placed them because *there is a contrast between them* of a very striking kind. The contrast is as instructive as the parallel.

The Parallel

Why do men become drunk with wine or other alcoholic liquors? The reasons are innumerable, but we can benefit from mentioning some of them.

One motive is *to find in wine exhilaration*. It is a holiday; let us have wine that we may warm our hearts and laugh and sing and make merry. It is a wedding day, a birthday, something out of the ordinary. Bring forth the wine cup! So say the sons of men. But when the man has drunk what he ought to think enough, he drinks yet more. Strong drink is taken to exhilarate, and for a while it has that effect. How some people are carried away when intoxicated! How lifted up they are! What a great man the least becomes! What a divine the man who never looked into his Bible! What a philosopher the boor who is without education! What a lord of creation the loon who has not two shirts! What a hero, every way, the coward who is afraid of his own shadow!

It is natural that we should all wish to be somewhat exhilarated. We like to have stirring times of pleasure, good times, and holidays. "Now," says the apostle, "that you may enjoy the most exquisite exhilaration, be filled with the Spirit." When the Spirit of God comes into a man with power so as to fill his soul, He brings to the man's soul a joy, a delight, an elevation of mind, a delightful and healthy excitement that lift him up above the dull dead-level of ordinary life and cause him to rejoice with joy unspeakable and full of glory.

I commend this exhilaration to you. It is safe delight because it is holy delight; holy delight because it is the Holy Spirit that works in you, and He makes you to delight in everything that is pleasing to the Holy God. One no longer needs to seek another source of excitement, for here is something more safe, more suitable, more sacred, more ennobling: "Be filled with the Spirit."

I know there are some Christians who never have much joy. Their experience is similar to the prodigal's elder brother as expressed to his father: "Lo, these many years do I serve thee, neither transgressed I at any time thy commandment: and yet thou never gavest me a kid, that I might make merry with my friends" (Luke 15:29). Far too many Christians are like that. "I have read my Bible, have acted consistently with my profession of faith, yet I know nothing of delight in God." Take this advice: "be filled with the Spirit." You have, as yet, received only a few drops from the divine shower of His sacred influences. Ask for the rivers, the floods, the torrents of His sacred power. Let the heavenly floods come in and fill you up to the brim and then will you have a joy that shall rival the bliss of those who are before the throne of God.

Furthermore, I know people who drink wine with the idea of being *strengthened* by it, despite the fact that the best physicians are telling us that there is no strength whatever in it. However faulty their reasoning, many indulge in wine to an extreme with the goal of obtaining strength. But to Christians the instruction comes, "be filled with the Spirit," for the Spirit of God can give you strength to the highest degree. He can gird you with spiritual strength—the strength of faith—and there is no strength like it, for all things are possible to him who believes. He can give strength that wrestles in prayer, that lays hold upon the Angel of the Covenant and will not let Him go except He grant a blessing. The Spirit of God gives the strength to suffer and the strength to labor, to receive and to give out again, to hope, to love, to conquer temptation, to perform holy action. When you are filled with the Spirit, how strong you are!

And though such a person may be in a place for only a short time, he leaves a fragrance behind that will not be forgotten. Whether you are a preacher or teacher or parent or someone engaged in the service of God in your ordinary labor, if you want strength with which to bring glory to the Most High, be filled with the Spirit!

Wine has been taken to excess to give people confidence, and it does that to a very high degree. A drunken man will do what he would never think of doing at any other time. He will be rash, foolhardy, and daring to the last degree. We have heard of nations whose troops have been so afraid to fight that they have dosed them with strong drink to induce them to march into the battle. No doubt many a man under the influence of drink has risked his life and performed what looked like feats of valor, when, indeed, he was simply out of his right mind or he would not have been so foolhardy. Wine does embolden many men in a wrong way. We are not to make ourselves ridiculous with fanaticism but are to make ourselves bold with the Spirit of truth. Be filled with the Spirit of the living God, wherein is quietness and whereof comes a courage that is to be admired. How brave a man is when he is filled with the Spirit of God! Then, knowing a thing to be right, he resolves to do it without counting the cost. He counted the cost long ago and reckoned that the light suffering that would come by doing right was no longer worthy to be compared with the glory of being found a faithful servant of God.

When a man is not filled with the Spirit of God, he begins calculating the financial cost. He says, "I know that what I am doing is wrong, but it would involve too much sacrifice to give it up." That man has little, if any, of the Spirit of God, for the Spirit destroys selfishness and love of gain. A man in whom the Spirit of God dwells abundantly says, "I shall never think, from this day forth, what may be the consequences of any course of action that the Lord my God commands me to follow. If it is right in the sight of God, I will do it. If God approves it, so shall it be; but if it is wrong, not a world made of gold—if it could all be mine—should tempt me."

Be filled with the Spirit. It will make you bold in the cause of the Lord Jesus. How bold the martyrs were! How bravely humble women were to speak for Christ! How slaves, peasants, and the uneducated faced the Roman governors—ay, stood before the Roman Emperor himself—and were not afraid! They were a brave people because they were filled with the Spirit. The Holy Spirit is the creator of heroes. If the Spirit of God departs, we are cowards; but if the Spirit of God shall come upon us, then every man and woman, however timid by nature, will be able to bear witness for Christ.

Wine also has been taken for *the elimination of pain*, for the drowning of misery, for support in the agony of cruel death. Solomon says, "Give strong drink unto him that is ready to perish, and wine unto those that be of heavy hearts. Let him drink, and forget his poverty, and remember his misery no more" (Prov. 31:6–7). It was an old custom that when a man was doomed and about to die, he was given some narcotic cup that he might suffer less. There was some mercy in this, though truly "the tender mercies of the wicked are cruel" (Prov. 12:10).

No doubt many people have most foolishly taken to drink to forget their grief and sorrow. To be filled with the Spirit is a holy and perfect way to remove depression and be sustained under anguish in a most wonderful way. If you want to forget your misery, ask for a sweet visitation of the Comforter. If some great calamity has come to you and you are saying, "How shall I bear it?," the answer is, "Be filled with the Spirit of God." Here shall you drink oblivion of the heavy trial, or better still, you shall forget the sharpness of the trial in the spiritual knowledge that trials work patience, and patience experience, and experience hope, which does not disappoint us.

Do not kick at the trial; be willing to bear it; but get more of the indwelling of the sacred Comforter. Seek earnestly for more of the Spirit of God than you ever had before. He will give you in proportion to your necessity. He is fully equal to every emergency. His consolations can balance your tribulations. Wait upon Him for the comfort of the Spirit. The day may come when you will glory in your weaknesses and afflictions because God used them to make room for more of His Spirit to dwell in you. When the Holy Spirit is given in a larger measure, you will have more happiness and be more content and a better person by reason of all this affliction. God grant that you may find it to be true. May you drink deep draughts of the joy of the Lord till you are filled with the Spirit of God!

I think a fifth reason why some have been drinking is to *arouse themselves*. They feel flat, they say. You can always find reasons for pursuing a course of self-indulgence: "I am rather down. I want something that will pick me up." By the time the person has had enough to drink, he feels worse than before. But if ever you feel dull, "be filled with the Spirit." Go to Him. You know His glorious name: He is the resurrection and the life. Look to Him for quickening, and it comes. Do not say, "I cannot pray today; I cannot sing today," but go to the Lord to help you to present acceptable worship. If you do not pray except when you feel like praying, you will not pray much, nor will you pray when you most need it. When you do not feel like doing the Lord's work, you must say, "Out with you, Mr. Sluggard! You must get to your work. Come Holy Spirit and fill me with power."

If the Spirit of God makes us feel what poor creatures we are and what a great Savior we have, if the Spirit of God makes us feel the love of God shed abroad in our hearts, if we burn with love to the souls of men, if we rejoice in the pardon bought with blood, if we see our justification and realize it, if we feel the Spirit of God melting us to tenderness or strengthening us to holy bravery—then it is that we are refreshed after the best manner. We have found the true arousing, and there will be no reaction after it, no falling back into a deeper depression.

Many men become drunkards from love of what is called *good fellowship*. Said a wife to her husband, "How can you drink as you do? Why, a hog would not do so." The wretched man replied, "No, I suppose a hog is more sensible than I am. But if there was another hog at the other side of the trough that said, 'I drink to your health,' this hog would be obliged to do the same. And if there were half a dozen of them toasting one another, I expect the hog would get as drunk as I am."

Sad are the effects of evil fellowship. Now see the beauty when the Spirit of God comes upon Christians, what fellowship they have with one another, what delight they take in holy conversation, what joy there is in meeting together for worship! Notice what comes after, "Speaking to yourselves in psalms and hymns and spiritual songs, singing and making melody in your heart to the Lord; Giving thanks always for all things unto God and the Father in the name of our Lord Jesus Christ" (Eph. 5:19–20). See the effect of being filled with the Spirit. It brings a fellowship of holy music, sacred gratitude, and heavenly thanksgiving. The Lord grant us grace to see our fellowship where He finds it, with holy men and women, that among them in joyous fellowship we may rejoice and praise His name.

The Contrast

I do not think that Paul was running the parallel only, for it would dishonor the work of the Holy Spirit to think that His operations could be in all things compared to the influence of alcohol. No, the divine influence far excels anything that earthly excitements can produce.

"Be not drunk with wine, wherein is excess; but be filled with the Spirit." The contrast is at the very beginning; for it is written, "Be *filled*." Wine does not fill. No man is satisfied with all that he drinks. His thirst is often increased rather being quenched. The Spirit of God has a satisfying, satiating influence upon the heart. It fills it to the very brim, until the man delights in God and cries, "My cup runneth over." Then the saint becomes like the tribe of which we read, "O Naphtali, satisfied with favour, and full with the blessing of the LORD" (Deut. 33:23). Wine ministers to lust, and lust is a burning sense of want; but the Spirit of the Lord brings fullness with it and a perfect rest of heart.

"Wine creates *riot*," says the apostle, and that is the second point of contrast. When men are drunk, what a noise they make! But the Holy Spirit, when you are full of Him, makes you quiet with a deep, unutterable peace. I do not say that you will not sing and rejoice, but there will be a deep calm within your spirit. I wish that some believers were filled with the Spirit if there were no other effect produced upon them but that of peace, self-possession, restfulness, and freedom from passion. I do not find any fault with those who bring with it a little noise, though the less of it the better. If your personality goes that way, sing unto the Lord and blow your trumpet; but at the same time, the solid people in the church are those who possess their souls, who go about their business, who endure and labor with an inward peace that is not disturbed, a holy calm that is not ruffled. Do not create riot, but abide in holy peace by being filled with the Spirit. May the Lord keep you in perfect peace.

The next point of contrast is that wine causes *contention*. How ready drunks are to quarrel! They make a harmless word to be an insult. Many a drunk is ready to fight anybody and everybody. But when you are filled with the Spirit, what is the result? Why, peaceful submission. Listen to this: "Submitting yourselves one to another in the fear of God. Wives, submit yourselves unto your own husbands, as unto the Lord" (Eph. 5:21–22). Human nature likes rule, but the Spirit of God works submissiveness of mind. Instead of wanting to be first, the truly spiritual man will be satisfied to be last if he can thus glorify God. That man who must always be king of the castle is not filled with the Spirit of God, but he who is willing to be a doormat on which the saints may wipe their feet is great in the kingdom of heaven. Be filled with the Spirit, and you will soon submit to inconvenience, mis-apprehensions, and even trials for the sake of doing good to those who are out of the way and in the hope of edifying the people of God. Wine causes riot; the Spirit causes peace. Drunkenness causes contention; the Spirit of God causes submission.

Furthermore, drunkenness makes men *foolish*, but the Spirit of God makes them wise. "See then that ye walk circumspectly, not as fools, but as wise" (Eph. 5:15). The drunken man cannot walk at all, often ending in a stagger till he falls. The man filled with the Spirit has a very definite idea of which way he is going. He knows the right way, and he deliberately chooses it; he perceives the straight and narrow way, and he steadfastly follows it, for God has made him wise. Folly clings to the wine cup, but wisdom comes with the Holy Spirit.

Drunkenness *wastes time*, but the Spirit of God helps us save time. "Redeeming the time, because the days are evil. Wherefore be ye not unwise, but understanding what the will of the Lord is" (Eph. 5:16–17). How much time is wasted over drink! But the child of God, when the Spirit of God enters into him, is made conscious of even his leisure minutes. As goldsmiths sweep up the very dust of their shops, that no filings of precious metal may be lost, so does the Spirit-filled believer make use of his briefest of intervals. It is wonderful what may be done in odd minutes. Little spaces of time may be made to yield a great harvest of usefulness and a rich revenue of glory to God!

Drunkenness makes men *forget their relationships*, but the Holy Spirit makes men remember them. The rest of the fifth chapter goes on to mention our relationships as wives, husbands, children, fathers, servants, masters. The drunken man is bad in every relationship, and the drunken woman is, if possible, worse. Selfishness eats up the very heart of those who otherwise might have been the objects of reverence and love. The contrast to this is the fact that when filled with the Spirit, the husband is the tenderest of husbands, the wife the best of wives. No master is so just as the man who is mastered by the Spirit of God; no servant so diligent as he that serves the Lord. By the Holy Spirit our relationships become ennobled, and what was but commonplace wears a glory of holiness about it. We are transfigured by the Spirit of God, and we transfigure everything we touch.

Lastly, excess of drink *leaves a person weak and exposed to peril.* But to be filled with the Spirit!—listen to what Ephesians 6:10–11 adds: "Finally, my brethren, be strong in the Lord, and in the power of his might. Put on the whole armour of God, that ye may be able to stand against the wiles of the devil." When filled with the Spirit, the man no longer lies upon the ground in danger as one overcome with wine. He is no longer open to the attack of adversaries as one who sleeps through strong drink. God has made him strong and armed him, and now he goes forth to fight in the service of his Master.

Be Filled with the Spirit

Our heart's desire is that the members of Christ's mystical body should be filled with the Spirit. Oh, that you may come absolutely under the sway of the Holy Ghost and may abide under His most powerful inspirations! Do you ask how this is to be? First, *reverently regard Him.* Worship Him. Speak not of the Holy Ghost as *it.* Talk not of the Third Person of the adorable Trinity as *an influence.* He is very God of very God. God has guarded the sanctity of the Holy Spirit by causing a certain sin to be specially condemned and excepted from pardon—the sin against the Holy Ghost. Honor Him much, then: worship Him, and adore Him, and look to Him for help.

Next, *do not grieve Him.* If there is anything that grieves the Holy Spirit, let it grieve *you* so that you may keep clear of it. Put away every thought, idea, principle, and act that is not agreeable to His mind. Neither live in sin, nor play with evil, nor fall into error, nor neglect the Word of God, nor fail to obey God's commands. Do not grieve the Comforter, but welcome Him as your best Friend. Open your heart to Him. Watch each day to hear His instructions. Pray every morning, "Holy Spirit, speak with me, enlighten me, set me on fire, dwell in me"; and during the day lament if the reality of His presence is not with you, and ask why it is so. Say—

> Return, O holy Dove! return,
> Sweet messenger of rest!
> I hate the sins that made thee mourn,

And drove thee from my breast.

As you welcome Him when He comes, so *be ready for Him to come* to you and dwell in you. Be clean, for He is pure. Do not expect the Holy Ghost to dwell in a foul chamber. You cannot make that chamber like Solomon's golden temple, but you can take care that it is well cleansed. Only the pure in heart shall see God. Oh, for a clean life, a clean tongue, a clean hand, a clean ear, a clean eye, a clean heart! God give you these, and then you shall be ready for the Spirit of God to dwell in you.

And when the Holy Spirit does come, learn this lesson. *If you would have Him fill you, obey Him.* If you believe that an impulse is from the Spirit of God, follow it out. Set the tone of your life by the tenderness of your conscience from the beginning. Do the Lord's will, whatever the consequences might be. Trials may be severe, but they will benefit your whole character. Follow truth wherever it leads and expect the Spirit of God to abide with you in so doing. Do not make compromises. If you take your hat off to the devil today, you will have to take your shoes off to him soon, and finally you will become his slave. Be strong for the truth. Stand fast for God and holiness. You will be filled with the Spirit if you are obedient to Him.

If you are filled with the Spirit of God and wish to retain His gracious presence, *speak about Him.* Note the curious word that follows "be filled with the Spirit; speaking. . . ." The Holy Ghost is not a dumb Spirit, He sets us "speaking to yourselves in psalms and hymns and spiritual songs, *singing* and making melody in your heart to the Lord." When the Spirit of God fills you, you will not only speak but also sing. Let the holy power have free course: do not quench the Spirit. If you feel like singing all the while, sing all the while, and let others know that there is a joy in the possession of the Spirit of God that the world does not understand but that you possess. Oh, that the Spirit of God would fill you to overflowing and place within you a fire that will set your church aflame!

Oh—let us blush to tell it—how often have we despised Him, resisted Him, and quenched the Spirit. He strove with us, but we strove against Him. But blessed be His dear name and let Him have everlasting worship for it, He would not let us go! We would not be saved, but He would save us. We sought to throw ourselves into the fire, but He sought to rescue us from the burning. He wrestled with us and held us fast. He would not let us destroy our souls. How did we scorn and scoff Him! How did we despise the Word that would lead us to Christ! How did we violate that holy cord that was gently drawing us to Jesus and His cross! I am sure, at the recollections of the persevering struggles of the Spirit with you, you must be stirred to love Him.

Chapter Eleven

Grieving the Holy Spirit

And grieve not the holy Spirit of God, whereby ye are sealed unto the day of redemption—Ephesians 4:30.

THERE IS SOMETHING VERY TOUCHING in this admonition, "Grieve not the Holy Spirit of God." It does not say, "Do not make Him angry." In selecting "grieve," a more delicate and tender term is used. Some people are so hard-hearted that to make another angry does not give them much pain, but where is the heart so hard that it is not moved when we know that we have caused others grief?—for grief is a sweet combination of anger and love. It is anger, but all bitterness has been removed. Love sweetens the anger and turns the edge of it, not against the person but against the offense.

How we make a practical distinction between the two terms is easily described. When I commit any offense, an acquaintance who has little patience is instantly angry with me. When a loving father observes the same offense, he is grieved. There is anger in his heart, but His anger is against my sin, and yet there is love to neutralize and modify his anger toward me. Instead of wishing me misfortune or pain as punishment of my sin, he looks upon my sin itself as being the ill. He grieves to think that I am already injured from the fact that I have sinned. I say this is a heavenly medicine, more precious than all the ointment of the merchants. There may be the bitterness of myrrh, but there is all the sweetness of frankincense in this sweet term *to grieve.*

To grieve anyone, even without a cause and without intention, causes a distress of heart where you do not want to rest until the grief has been dealt with—till you have made some explanation or apology and have done your best to remedy the pain and take away the grief. When we see anger in another, we immediately feel hostility. Anger begets anger, but grief begets pity, and pity is next akin to love, and we love those whom we have caused to grieve. Now, is this not a very sweet expression, "Grieve not the Holy Spirit"? The emotion here described is that of grief to the Holy Spirit of God. And is it not a tender and touching thing that the Holy Spirit should direct His servant Paul to say to us to not excite His loving anger, to not vex Him, to not cause Him to mourn? He is a dove; do not cause Him to mourn because you have treated Him harshly and ungratefully.

The Love of the Spirit

To consider the love of the Holy Spirit presses us forward to not grieve the Spirit, for when we are persuaded that another loves us, we find at once a very powerful reason why we should not grieve Him. The love of the Spirit! Surely it requires a songster to sing it, for love is to be spoken of only in words of song. The love of the Spirit! Let me tell you of His early love to us. He loved us without beginning. In the eternal covenant of grace, all that can be said of the love of the Father and of the love of the Son may be said of the love of the Spirit—it is eternal, infinite, sovereign, everlasting; it is a love that cannot be dissolved, decreased, or removed from those who are objects of it.

But permit me to refer you to His acts rather than His attributes. Let me tell you of the love of the Spirit to you and to me. How early was that love that He manifested toward us, even in our childhood. It is good to recall how early the Spirit of God spoke to our conscience and solemnly convicted us of youthful sins. How frequently since then has the Spirit wooed us! How often under the ministry of His Word has He compelled our hearts to melt, and the tear has run down our cheeks and He has sweetly whispered in our ear, "My child, give Me your heart; shut yourself into Me, confess your sins, and seek a Savior's love and blood."

Oh—let us blush to tell it—how often have we despised Him, resisted Him, and quenched the Spirit. He strove with us, but we strove against Him. But blessed be His dear name and let Him have everlasting worship for it, He would not let us go! We would not be saved, but He would save us. We sought to throw ourselves into the fire, but He sought to rescue us from the burning. He wrestled with us and held us fast. He would not let us destroy our souls.

How did we scorn and scoff Him! How did we despise the Word that would lead us to Christ! How did we violate that holy cord that was gently drawing us to Jesus and His cross! I am sure, at the recollections of the persevering struggles of the Spirit with you, you must be stirred to love Him. How often did He restrain you from sin, even when you were about to plunge headlong into a course of wickedness! If it had not been for that sweet Holy Spirit, you would not have been prepared for meeting the Lord. Though you were like an oxen unaccustomed to the yoke, yet He would not let you have your way. He would not throw the reins upon your neck. But He said, "I will have him; I will change his heart; I will not let him go till I have made him mine."

And then, consider that blessed moment when the Holy Spirit guided you to Jesus. Do you remember the love of the Spirit when He took you aside and showed you Jesus on the tree? Who was it that opened your blind eye to see a dying Savior? Who opened your deaf ear to hear the voice of pardoning love? Who opened your paralyzed hand to receive the gifts of a Savior's grace? Who was it that broke the hardness of your heart and made a way for the Savior to enter and dwell in? It was that precious Spirit, the same Spirit whom you despised and resisted in the days of your flesh. What a mercy it was that He did not say, "I will swear in my wrath that they shall not enter into my rest, for they have vexed me" or "Ephraim is joined unto idols, I will let him alone!"

And since that time, how sweetly has the Spirit proved His love to you and me. It is not only His first strivings and His divine quickenings, but throughout our life, how much have we owed to His instruction. We have been slow learners from God's Word and retained but little. How little progress have we made in the school of grace! We are still learners, unstable, weak, and apt to fall, but what a blessed instructor we have had! Has He not led us into many truths and taken the things of Christ and applied them to us?

When I think how stupid I have been, I wonder that He has not given me up. When I think what an idiot I have been, when He would have taught me the things of the kingdom of God, I marvel that He should have had such patience with me. Is it a wonder that Jesus should become a babe? Is it not an equal wonder that the Spirit of the living God should become the teacher of babes? It is a marvel that Jesus should lie in a manger. Is it not an equal marvel that the Holy Spirit should usher us into the sacred school to teach fools and make them wise? It was condescension that brought the Savior to the cross. Is it not equal condescension that brings the mighty Spirit of grace down to dwell with stubborn and unruly sinners, to teach them the mystery of the kingdom, and to make them know the wonders of a Savior's love?

Remember how much we owe to the Spirit's consolation, how much He has manifested His love in cherishing us in all our sicknesses, assisting us in all our labors, and comforting us in all our distresses. I can testify what a blessed comforter He has been to me. When every other comfort failed, when the promise itself seemed empty, when the ministry was void of power, it was then that the Holy Spirit proved a rich comfort to my soul and filled my poor heart with peace and joy in believing.

How many times would your heart have broken if the Spirit had not bound it up? How often has He who is your teacher also become your physician, closing the wounds of your poor bleeding spirit and binding up those wounds with the ministry of His promises, and so has given you back your spiritual health? It is a marvel that the Holy Ghost should become a comforter, for comforting is considered an inferior work by many people in the church. To teach, to preach, to command with authority—how many are willing to do this because this is impressive work. But to sit down and bear with the sins and weaknesses of the creature, to enter into all the stratagems of unbelief, to help the soul find a way of peace in the midst of seas of trouble—this is compassion like a God, that the Holy Spirit should stoop from heaven to become a comforter of hopeless spirits. What! Must He Himself wait upon His sick child and stay by his bed? Must He make his bed for him in his affliction? Must He carry him in his infirmity? Must He breathe continually into him His very breath? Does the Holy Spirit become a waiting servant of the church? Does He become a lamp to enlighten? Does He become a staff on which we may lean? These abundant proofs of His love should move us to love the Holy Spirit.

Yet there are larger fields beyond that speak of the love of the Spirit. Consider how much He loves us when He helps our weaknesses. Not only does He help our weaknesses, but even when we do not know how to pray, He teaches us. And when "we ourselves groan within ourselves" (Rom. 8:23), the Spirit Himself makes intercession for us with groanings that cannot be uttered—so that our prayer reaches the ears of Christ, and is then presented before His Father's face. To *help* our weaknesses is a wonderful love, but when God overcomes them altogether or removes them, there is something very noble and grand and sublime in the deed. When He permits the weakness to remain and yet works with the weakness, there is tender compassion indeed. When the Savior heals the lame man, you see His Godhead; but when He walks with the lame man, limping though his gait may be, when He sits with the beggar, when He talks with the publican, when He carries the babe in His bosom—this helping of weaknesses is a manifestation of love almost unequalled. Apart from Christ's bearing our sins in His own body on the tree, I know of no greater or more tender instance of divine love than when it is written, "Likewise the Spirit also helpeth our infirmities" (Rom. 8:26).

How much you owe to the Spirit when you have been on your knees in prayer! You know what it is to be dull and lifeless there, to groan for a word and not find it, to wish for a word and yet the very wish is weary, to long to have desires and yet all the desire you have is a desire that you may be able to desire. Have you sometimes, when your desires have been kindled, longed to get a grip at the promise by the hand of faith, but the promise was beyond your reach. If you touched it with the tip of your finger, you could not grasp it as you desired, you could not plead it, and therefore you came away without the blessing. But when the Spirit has helped our weakness, how we have prayed! There have been times when I have so grasped the knocker of the gate of mercy and have let it fall with such tremendous force that it seemed as if the very gate shook and tottered. There have been seasons when we have laid hold upon the Angel of the Covenant, have overcome heaven by prayer, have declared we would not let Jehovah Himself go except He bless us. We have moved the hand that moves the world. We have brought down upon us the eyes that look upon the universe. All this we have done, not by our own strength but by the might and power of the Spirit.

Another marvel of the Spirit's love remains—namely, His indwelling the saints. We sing in one of our hymns, "Dost thou not dwell in all the saints?" We ask a question that can have but one answer: He does dwell in the heart of all God's redeemed and blood-washed people. What a condescension is this—that He whom the heaven of heavens cannot contain, dwells in your heart. That heart so agitated with anxious care and thoughts, too often defiled with sin, and yet He dwells there. The little narrow heart of man the Holy Spirit has made His palace. When I think how often I have let the devil in, I wonder that the Spirit has not withdrawn.

The final perseverance of the saints is one of the greatest miracles on record. In fact, it is the sum total of miracles. The perseverance of a saint for a single day is a multitude of miracles of mercy. When you consider that the Spirit is of purer eyes than to behold iniquity, and yet He dwells in the heart where sin often intrudes, a heart out of which comes all manner of evil, what if sometimes He were grieved and were to leave us to ourselves for a season? It is a marvel that He is there at all, for He must be grieved with those base intruders who thrust themselves into that little temple that He had honored with His presence.

Yes, let us love Jesus with all our hearts, but let us not forget to love the Holy Spirit, too. Let us have songs for Him, worship for Him. You talk of the love, grace, tenderness, and faithfulness of Christ. Why do you not say the same of the Spirit? Was there ever love like His, ever mercy like His, ever faithfulness like His, that multitudes of sins cannot drive Him away? Was ever power like His that overcomes all our iniquities and yet leads us safely on, though hosts of foes within and without would rob us of our Christian life?

Unto His name be glory forever and ever.

It Is by the Holy Spirit We Are Sealed

Here we have another reason why *we should not grieve the Spirit*: by whom we "are sealed unto the day of redemption." The Spirit Himself is expressed as the seal, even as He Himself is directly said to be the pledge of our inheritance. The sealing, I think, has a threefold meaning. It is a sealing of *attestation* or confirmation. I want to know whether I am truly a child of God. The Spirit bears witness with my spirit that I am born of God. I have the writings, the title deeds of the inheritance that is to come—I want to know whether those are valid or whether they are mere counterfeits written out by that old scribe of hell, Master Presumption and Carnal Security. How am I to know? I look for the seal of the Holy Spirit. Faith that is unsealed may be a poison, it may be presumption, but faith that is sealed by the Spirit is true, real, genuine faith. Never be content unless you are sealed by the inward witness and testimony of the Holy Ghost. It is possible for a person to know beyond a doubt that he is secure of heaven—by being able with the eye of faith to see the seal, the stamp of the Holy Spirit set upon his own character and experience. It is a seal of attestation.

The sealing is also a sealing of *appropriation*. It is common for men to put their mark upon an article to show that it is their own. So the Holy Spirit puts His mark upon the hearts of all His people. He seals us. "They shall be mine," says the Lord, "in that day when I make up my jewels" (Mal. 3:17). And then the Spirit puts God's seal upon us to signify that we are God's reserved inheritance—His peculiar people, the portion in which His soul delights.

Again, by sealing is meant *preservation*. Men seal up that which they wish to have preserved, and when a document is sealed it becomes valid. It is by the Spirit of God that the Christian is sealed, that he is kept, preserved, sealed until Christ comes fully to redeem the bodies of His saints by raising them from the dead and fully to redeem the world by purging it from sin and making it a kingdom unto Himself in righteousness. We are saved by the sealing of the Spirit. Apart from that we perish. When the last general fire shall blaze out, everything without the seal of the Spirit shall be burned up. But those who are sealed, mounting above the flames, shall dwell with Christ eternally and sing the everlasting song of gratitude and praise. This is the second reason why we should love the Spirit and why we should not grieve Him.

The Grieving of the Spirit

How may we grieve the Spirit? I am now referring to those who love the Lord Jesus Christ. The Spirit of God is in your heart, and it is very, very easy indeed to grieve Him. Sin is as easy as it is wicked. You may grieve Him by impure thoughts. He cannot bear sin. If you indulge in lustful thoughts and allow your imagination to be captured by them, if your heart goes after covetousness, if you set your heart upon anything that is evil, the Spirit of God will be grieved in this way: "I love this man, I want his heart, and yet he is entertaining these filthy lusts. His thoughts, instead of running after me, and after Christ and the Father, are running after the temptations that are in the world through lust." And then His Spirit is grieved. He sorrows in His soul because He knows what sorrow these things must bring to our souls.

We grieve Him yet more if we indulge in outward acts of sin. Then is He sometimes so grieved that He takes His flight for a season, for the dove will not dwell in our hearts if we take filth and sin in there. If we commit sin, if we openly bring disgrace upon our Lord, if we tempt others to follow our example, it is not long before the Holy Spirit will begin to grieve. If we neglect prayer, if we forget to read the Scriptures, if we never seek to do any good in the world, if we live merely for ourselves and not to Christ, the Holy Spirit will be grieved, for thus He says, "They have forsaken me the fountain of living waters, and hewed out cisterns, broken cisterns" (Jer. 2:13).

I think I now see the Spirit of God grieving when you say you have no time for prayer but the Spirit sees you very active with worldly things and having many hours to spare for relaxation and amusement. And then He is grieved because He sees that you love worldly things better than you love Him. His spirit is grieved within Him. Take care that He does not go away from you, for it will be a pitiful thing for you if He leaves you to yourself.

Ingratitude also tends to grieve Him. Nothing cuts a man to the heart more than after having done his utmost for another, he turns around and repays him with ingratitude or insult. When the Holy Spirit looks into our soul and sees little love for Christ, no gratitude to Him for all He has done for us, is He grieved.

The Holy Spirit is exceedingly grieved by our unbelief. When we distrust the promise He has given and applied, when we doubt the power or the affection of our blessed Lord, the Spirit says within Himself: "They doubt My truthfulness; they distrust My power; they say Jesus is not able to save them"; thus again is the Spirit grieved. I wish the Spirit had an advocate beside you who could speak in better terms than I have. It is a theme that overpowers me; I seem to grieve for Him, but I cannot make you grieve or describe the grief I feel. Yet in my own soul I keep saying, "This is exactly what I have done—I have grieved Him, too." Much within us has made that sacred Dove to mourn, and my marvel is that He has not taken His flight from us and left us utterly to ourselves.

Now suppose the Holy Spirit is grieved, *what is the effect produced upon us*? When the Spirit is first grieved, He bears with us. He is grieved again and again, and again and again, and still He bears with it all. But at last His grief becomes so excessive that He says, "I will suspend My operations; I will leave life behind Me, but My own actual presence I will take away." And when the Spirit of God goes away from the soul, what a miserable state we are in. He suspends His instructions; we read the Word, we cannot understand it; we go to our commentaries, they cannot tell us the meaning; we fall on our knees and ask to be taught, but we get no answer, we learn nothing. He suspends His comfort. We used to dance like David before the ark, and now we sit like Job in the ash heap and scrape our ulcers with a potsherd. There was a time when His candle shone around us, but now He is gone; He has left us in the blackness of darkness. Now He takes from us all spiritual power. Once we could do all things; now we can do nothing. We could slay the Philistines; but now Delilah can deceive us and our eyes are put out and we are made to grind in the mill. We go preaching, but there is no pleasure in preaching, and no good follows it. There is the machinery, but there is no love. There is the intention to do good—or perhaps not even that—but alas, there is no power to accomplish the intention! The Lord has withdrawn Himself; His light, joy, comfort, spiritual power—all are gone.

When the Spirit goes away, faith shuts up like a flower; no perfume is exhaled. Then the fruit of our love begins to rot and drops from the tree. Then the sweet buds of our hope become frostbitten and die. What a sad thing it is to lose the Spirit. Have you never been on your knees and realized that the Spirit of God was not with you, and what awful work it has been to groan and cry and sigh and yet go away again without a light to shine upon the promises, not so much as a ray of light through the chink of the dungeon. All forsaken, forgotten, and forlorn, you are almost driven to despair. You sing with Cowper:

> What peaceful hours I once enjoyed,
> How sweet their memory still!
> But they have left an aching void,
> The world can never fill.
>
> Return, Thou sacred dove, return,
> Sweet messenger of rest,
> I hate the sins that made Thee mourn,
> And drove Thee from my breast.
>
> The dearest idol I have known,
> Whate'er that idol be,
> Help me to tear it from its throne,
> And worship only Thee.

Ah, it is sad enough to have the Spirit drawn from us! But there are whole churches that are very much in the position of those who have grieved the Spirit of God, for the Spirit deals with churches just as it does with individuals. In recent years, how few sinners were brought to Christ, how empty our places of worship have become. Our prayer meetings dwindle away to nothing, and our church meetings are a farce. But the saddest part is that the churches are willing to have it so. They do not even care whether revival comes to their members or not. Something has been done that has driven the Spirit of God from these churches. The Holy Spirit is grieved, and He is gone. Church members need to humble themselves before God and cry aloud that He will visit His church and that He would open the windows of heaven and pour out His grace upon His thirsty hill of Zion, that sinners may be saved by the thousands. Let us cry aloud to the Holy Spirit, who is certainly grieved with His church, and let us purge our churches of everything that is contrary to His Word and to sound doctrine, and the Spirit will return and His power shall be manifest.

In conclusion, there may be some readers who have so grieved the Spirit that He has gone. It is a mercy for you to know that the Spirit of God never leaves His people finally. He leaves them for chastisement, but not for damnation. He sometimes leaves them that they may improve by knowing their own weakness, but He will not leave them finally to perish. Are you in a state of backsliding and coldness? Hearken to this solemn caution: stay not a moment in a condition so perilous; do not rest for a single second in the absence of the Holy Ghost.

I beseech you to use every means by which that Spirit may be brought back to you. Search yourself for the sin that has grieved the Spirit, give it up, slay that sin upon the spot. Repent with tears and sighs, continue in prayer, and never rest satisfied until the Holy Ghost comes back to you. Participate in a sincere ministry, fellowship with sincere believers, but above all, be often in prayer and let your daily cry be, "Return, return, O Holy Spirit return and dwell in my soul." I beseech you to not be content till that prayer is heard, for you are as weak as water and faint and empty while the Spirit has been away from you. Yield to Him, listen to Him, and obey Him as He moves you. I beseech you, do not despise Him.

Have you resisted Him many times? Then take care you do not again, for there may come a last time when the Spirit says,

"I will go unto my rest, I will not return unto him; the ground is accursed, it shall be given up to barrenness." Listen to the word of the gospel, for the Spirit speaks effectually to you in this short sentence: "Repent ye therefore, and be converted, that your sins may be blotted out, when the times of refreshing shall come from the presence of the Lord" (Acts 3:19).

May the Lord grant that we not grieve the Holy Spirit.

How should we approach prayer? By the book? Without book? In public? In private? By the way? In the house? On your knees? Standing? Sitting? Kneeling? Nothing is said about these; posture, place, and time are all left open. There is only one specific given—"in the Holy Ghost." That is indispensable. If that is in place, nothing else matters.

Chapter Twelve

Praying in the Holy Ghost

Praying in the Holy Ghost—Jude 20.

THE CONTEXT FOR THE APOSTLE'S WORDS in this passage is a contrasting of the ungodly and the godly. The ungodly are mocking, speaking great swelling words, and walking after their ungodly lusts, while the righteous are building up themselves in their most holy faith and keeping themselves in the love of God. The ungodly are showing the venom of their hearts by mourning and complaining, while the righteous are manifesting the new principle within them by "praying in the Holy Ghost." As the spider is said to find poison in the very flowers from which bees suck honey, so do the wicked abuse to sin the same mercies that the godly use to the glory of God. As far as light is removed from darkness and life from death, so far does a believer differ from the ungodly. Let us keep this contrast very vivid. While the wicked grow yet more wicked, let us become more holy, more prayerful, and more devout, saying with good old Joshua, "Let others do as they will, but as for me and my house, we will serve the Lord."

Note carefully the specific order in the context. The righteous are described, first of all, as building themselves up in their most holy faith. Faith is the first grace, the root of devotion, the foundation of holiness, the dawn of godliness. What, then, follows at the heels of faith? What is faith's firstborn child? When the vine of faith becomes vigorous and produces fruit unto holiness, which is the first ripe cluster? Is it not prayer—"praying in the Holy Ghost"? A prayerless man has no faith, and the man who abounds in faith will soon abound in supplication. Faith the mother and prayer the child are seldom apart from one another; faith carries prayer in her arms, and prayer draws life from the breast of faith. Edification in faith leads to fervency in supplication. Elijah first manifests his faith before the priests of Baal and then retires to wrestle with God upon Carmel.

What is it that follows after "praying in the Holy Ghost"? "Keep yourselves in the love of God" (Jude 21). Next to prayer comes an abiding sense of the love of God for us and the flowing up of our love toward God. Prayer builds an altar and lays the sacrifice and the wood in order, and then love, like the priest, brings holy fire from heaven and sets the offering in a blaze. Faith is the root of grace, prayer is the lily's stalk, and love is the spotless flower. Faith sees the Savior, prayer follows Him into the house, but loves breaks the alabaster box of precious ointment and pours it on His head. There is, however, a step beyond even the hallowed enjoyments of love. There remains a topstone to complete the building; it is believing expectancy—"looking for the mercy of our Lord Jesus Christ unto eternal life" (Jude 21). Farseeing hope climbs the staircase that hope has built and, bowing upon the knees of prayer, looks through the window that love has opened and sees the Lord Jesus Christ coming in His glory and endowing all His people with the eternal life that is to be theirs. See, then, the value of prayer as indicating the possession of faith and as foreshadowing and supporting the strength and growth of love.

Coming to the text, the apostle mentions only one kind of praying. Viewed from a certain point, prayers are of many sorts. I suppose that no two genuine prayers from different people could be precisely alike. As the author of prayer, the Holy Spirit does not often produce two prayers that are precisely the same upon the tablets of His people's hearts. Prayers may be divided in several different orders. There is prayer in which we plead for deliverance from the wrath of God. There are prayers in which we supplicate blessings and implore mercies from the liberal hand of God and entreat our heavenly Father to supply our needs out of His riches in glory in Christ Jesus. There are personal prayers, intercessory prayers, public or private prayers, vocal or mental prayers, lengthy or brief prayers. Prayers may be salted with confession or perfumed with thanksgiving. Prayers may be sung to music or wept out with groanings. The varieties of prayer are as many as are the flowers of summer.

There is one aspect, though, that prayers must all have in common if they are to be acceptable to God—they must be "in the Holy Ghost." Prayer that is not in the Holy Ghost is in the flesh, and that which is born of the flesh is flesh and cannot please God. A defiled and marred nature cannot be acceptable with the most Holy God. If the heavens are not pure in His sight, how shall those prayers that are born of the earth be acceptable to Him? The seed of acceptable devotion must come from heaven's storehouse. Only the prayer that comes from God can go to God. The desire that He writes upon our heart will move His heart and bring down a blessing, but the desires of the flesh have no power with Him.

The True Test of Our Prayers

How can we discern whether our prayers are true or not? Use the text as a crucible by which an accurate test can be made— have they truly been in "praying in the Holy Ghost"?

This test can be applied to those who have been in the habit of using *a form of prayer*. You perhaps would not dare go out to your day's business without having repeated that form at the breakfast table; you would be afraid to fall asleep at night without going through the words that you have set yourself to repeat. May I put the question to you, and will you try to answer it honestly: Have you prayed in the Holy Ghost? Has the Holy Spirit had anything to do with that form? Has He really placed this prayer in your heart? Is it not probable that there may be no heart whatever in it, and not an atom of sincerity? Is it not possible that you have mocked God with a solemn sound upon a thoughtless tongue? It is possible to spend an entire lifetime punctually performing our devotion by the use of a book or of a learned form and to never once have prayed at all. The whole of that period we may have been living in God's esteem an ungodly, prayerless life because we have never worshipped God in spirit and in truth and have never prayed in the Holy Ghost. Judge yourself that you be not judged.

The same test is as easily applied to spontaneous prayers. While they require some thought, they still may be heartless. They may simply represent a fluency in prayer acquired by practice that one's speech may ripple on for five or ten minutes and yet the heart may be wandering in vanity and spiritually stagnant. The body may be on its knees while the soul is on its wings far away from the mercy seat.

Let us examine our public prayers by the same standard. If a minister considers public prayer as merely his official duty to conduct the devotions of the congregation, he has much to account for before God. To lead the church in prayer without seeking the aid of the Holy Ghost is no light sin. And what shall be said of the prayers at prayer meetings? Are not many of them mere words? It is better to not speak at all rather than speak in the flesh. I am sure that the only prayer in which the devoted hearer can unite—and which is acceptable with God—is that which really is a heart prayer, a soul prayer, in fact, a prayer that the Holy Ghost moves us to pray. All else is beating the air and occupying time in vain.

We also need to consider our more private prayers, our supplications with our families, and, above all, our personal devotional life. We might discover our prayers far poorer things than we thought. There are times when it is a sweet and blessed thing to lay hold of the horns of the altar and to feel that the blood that sprinkles the altar has sprinkled you, that you have spoken to God and prevailed. It is a blessed thing to grasp the Angel of the Covenant and to wrestle with Him even hour after hour, saying, "I will not let You go unless You bless me"; but I fear these are rare occurrences.

Come, put your prayers into this crucible of "praying in the Holy Ghost," and how much straw and chaff will there be! Come and look through this window at the fields of our devotions, overgrown with nettles and thistles, a wilderness of merely outward performances, and how small that little spot, enclosed by grace, that the Holy Spirit has cleared, plowed and planted, from which the fruit of prayer has been brought forth unto perfection! May our heavenly Father teach us to be humble in His presence, allowing His searching eye to test our works, and may we come to Him afresh and ask Him to fill us with His Spirit.

A Reason for Gladness

It is a delightful reflection that God observes His people and does not sit as an indifferent spectator of their conflicts and difficulties. For instance, He closely observes us in our prayers. He knows that prayer, while it should be the easiest thing in the world, is not so. He knows that we do not always find it easy to approach Him in the true spirit of supplication, and He observes this with compassion. That is a precious verse for those hearts that are weak and broken: "He knoweth our frame: he remembereth that we are dust" (Ps. 103:14); and that other: "Like as a father pitieth his children, so the LORD pitieth them that fear him" (Ps. 103:13). He knows our frailties and failures in prayer; He sees His child fall as it tries to walk and marks the tears with which it bemoans its weakness. "The eyes of the Lord are upon the righteous, and his ears are open unto their cry" (Ps. 34:15).

A sweeter thought remains in the text—namely, that having considered our failures, our Lord is not angry with us but instead is moved to pity for us and love toward us. Instead of shutting the gates of mercy, He devises ways to bring the lame and the banished into His presence. He teaches the ignorant how to pray and strengthens the weak with His own strength. That help is not to be found in a book or in the repetition of certain words in certain consecrated places, but *in the condescending assistance of the Holy Spirit.*

I understand from the expression "praying in the Holy Ghost" that the Holy Ghost is actually willing to help me to pray, that He will tell me how to pray, and that when I get to a point where I am at a loss for words and cannot express my desires, He will appear in my extremity and make intercession in me with groaning that cannot be uttered. Jesus in His agony was strengthened by an angel; you are to be strengthened by God

Himself. This thought needs no adorning of oratorical expression. Take it as a wedge of gold of Ophir and value it; it is priceless, beyond all price. God Himself the Holy Ghost condescends to assist you when you are on your knees, and if you cannot put two words together in common speech to men, yet He will help you to speak with God. And if at the mercy seat you fail in words, you shall not fail in reality, for your heart shall conquer. God requires no words. He never reads our petitions according to the outward expression but reads them according to the inward groaning. He notices the longing, the desiring, the sighing, the crying.

Remember that the outward of prayer is but the shell; the inward of prayer is its true kernel and essence. Indeed, a prayer wailed forth in the bitter cry of anguish from a desolate spirit— a cry so discordant to human ears—is music to the ear of God. Notice the value of the heart in prayer, and be comforted.

How Then Shall We Pray?

How should we approach prayer? By the book? Without book? In public? In private? By the way? In the house? On your knees? Standing? Sitting? Kneeling? Nothing is said about these; posture, place, and time are all left open. There is only one specific given—"*in the Holy Ghost.*" That is indispensable. If that is in place, nothing else matters.

What does praying in the Holy Ghost mean? It may be translated *by* or *through* or *in* the Holy Ghost, and the phrase means, first, *praying in the Holy Ghost's power*. The carnal mind knows nothing about this. But those who are born of the Spirit are aware of the communications between their spirits and the Holy Spirit who is now resident in the midst of the church of God. We know that the Divine Spirit, without the use of sounds, speaks in our hearts, that without an utterance that the ear can hear, He can make our soul know His presence and understand His meaning. He casts the spiritual shadow of His influence over us, coloring our thoughts and feelings according to His own design and will.

It is a great spiritual fact that the Divine Spirit has frequent dealings with spiritual minds and imparts to them of His power.

Our newborn spirit has a certain degree of power in it, but the power is never fully manifested or drawn out unless the Spirit of God quickens our spirit and excites its activity. Our spirit prays, but it is because it is overshadowed and filled with the power of the Holy Ghost. If, in coming before the throne of heavenly grace, God's Eternal Spirit speaks to my soul and brings it up to be filled with divine force, if that Spirit is in me a well of water springing up into everlasting life, if I receive that divine light and power of the Holy Ghost, and if in His power I fervently draw near to God, my prayer must be prevalent with God. This power may be possessed by every Christian. May God grant it to all of His people that they may all pray in the Spirit! That, I think, is one meaning of the text—praying in the power of the Spirit.

No doubt the principal sense of the text is praying according to the mind of the Spirit. We do not always know what to pray for, and if we were to refrain from prayer for a few minutes till we did know, it would be a good and wise rule. Should we not wait upon God in prayer, asking Him to reveal to us what those matters are concerning which we should petition Him. Beware of hit-or-miss prayers. Never make haphazard work of supplication. Come to the throne of grace, intelligently understanding what it is that you require. It is well with us in prayer when the Holy Ghost guides the mind. Spiritual men can consciously sense a freedom or a restriction in the direction of their prayers; then let them obey the Holy Spirit and pray as He directs.

The secret is to pray for what God the Spirit moves you to pray for and to be very sensitive to the Holy Spirit's influence. Oh, that His faintest breath should cause a ripple upon the sea of our soul and move us as the Spirit would have it. We do not pray correctly if we think what it is *we* want and *we* wish for and then ask for it in selfish willfulness, but we pray correctly when we consent to that which is the mind of the Spirit. Lord, teach us to pray. Put Your thoughts into our minds, the desires into our hearts, and the very words into our lips, that we may be praying in the Spirit and not in the flesh.

The main part of praying in the Spirit also lies in the Spirit's assisting us *in the manner.* Observe the many ways there are of praying that are obnoxious to God; observe them and avoid them. He who comes to God must remember that He is "a Spirit: and they that worship him must worship him in spirit and in truth" (John 4:24), "for the Father seeketh such to worship him" (John 4:23). The first essential of prayer is to pray *in truth*, and we do not pray in truth unless the Spirit of God leads us into the sincerity and reality of devotion. To pray in truth is to mean what we say. It is for the heart to agonize with God and swell with strong desires, and where will you obtain such a manner of prayer except in the spiritual man moved by the Holy Ghost? The carnal man can chant a prayer and copy a form, but he is not praying. Only the spiritual man can sigh and long and cry in his inmost heart and in the chamber of his soul before God, and he will not do it unless the Spirit of truth leads him in sincerity into the secret of heart prayer.

Praying in the Holy Ghost is praying in *fervency*. Never ask the Lord to hear cold prayers. Those who do not plead with fervency do not plead at all. And lukewarm prayer will never do; it is essential that prayer be red-hot. Real prayer is burnt as with a hot iron into a man's soul and then comes forth from the man's soul like coals of juniper that have a furious heat. Such prayers are given only by the Holy Ghost. I have heard prayers with such power that I was bowed down in humiliation and then upborne as on the wings of eagles in the power of supplication. There is a way of praying with power in which a man seems to get hold of the posts of heaven's gate, as Samson grasped the pillars of the temple, and appears as though he would pull all down upon himself sooner than miss the blessing. That is praying in the Holy Ghost. May we be tutored in the art of offering effectual fervent prayer!

It is also essential in prayer that we pray with *perseverance*. To run fast for a short distance is easy, but to keep it up mile after mile is a battle. Similarly, some believers can pray very fervently now and then, but to continue in prayer—who shall do this except the Spirit of God sustains him? Mortal spirits flag and tire. The course of mere fleshly devotion is a course like a snail that melts as it crawls. Carnal minds go onward, and their devotion grows smaller by degrees and miserably less as they cry out, "What a weariness it is!" But when the Holy Ghost fills a man and leads him into prayer, the man gathers force as he proceeds and grows more fervent even when God delays to answer. The longer the gate is closed, the more vehemently the man uses the knocker till he thunders in his prayer. Beautiful in God's sight is tearful and yet unconquerable importunity. Surely we must have the Holy Spirit to help us prevail in prayer.

Another aspect of praying in the Spirit involves a *holy* frame of mind. Distractions to prayer frequently fill believers' minds. You sense the Lord's presence, but then some silly gossip causes your mind to wander. The recollection of a child at home or the remembrance of what somebody said six weeks ago will perplex your mind so that you cannot pray. But when the Holy Spirit comes, He takes a scourge of small cords and drives these buyers and sellers out of the temple, leaving it clear for God, and then you can come with a holy, devout frame of mind, fixed and settled in your great object of approach to God. This is to approach Him in the Spirit. Oh, for more of this blessed, undisturbed devotion!

I could not, however, finish the description of praying in the Spirit if I did not say that it means praying *humbly*, for the Holy Spirit never puffs us up with pride. He convinces us of sin and bows us down in contrition and brokenness of spirit. We must pray before God like the humble publican, or we shall never go forth justified as He was. We shall never sing *Gloria in excelsis* except we pray to God *De profundis*; out of the depths must we cry, or we shall never see the glory in the highest.

True prayer must be *loving* prayer if it is praying in the Holy Ghost. Prayer should be perfumed with love, saturated with love—love for our fellow believers and love for Christ. Moreover, it must be prayer full of *faith*. The effectual fervent prayer of a man prevails only as the man believes in God, and the Holy Spirit is the author of faith in us and nurtures and strengthens our faith so that we pray believing God's promise. Oh, that this blessed combination of excellent graces, priceless and sweet as the spices of the merchant, might be fragrant within us because the Holy Ghost's power is shed abroad in our hearts!

The Assurance of Prayer

Praying in the Spirit brings with it an absolute certainty that I must succeed with God in prayer. If my prayer were my own prayer, I might not be so sure of it, but if the prayer that I utter is God's own prayer written on my soul, what He writes on the heart is written there only because it is written in His purposes. It is said by an old divine that prayer is the shadow of Omnipotence. Our will, when God the Holy Spirit influences it, is the indicator of God's will. When God's people pray, it is because the blessing is coming, and their prayers are the shadow of the coming blessing.

Rest assured, God never contradicted in one place what He said in another. What He promised yesterday, He fulfills today, and what He said in one place, He declares in another. Then if God says in my heart, "Pray for So-and-so," it is because He has said it in the book of His decrees. The Spirit of God's writing in the heart always concurs with the writing of destiny in the book of God's eternal purpose. Rest assured that you cannot but succeed when you have laid your soul like a sheet of paper before God and asked Him to write upon it. Then it becomes the Spirit making intercession in you according to the will of God. He will do it—He is pledged to do it. If the Spirit teaches you to pray, it is certain that God will give you what you are seeking.

A Chariot to God

It is delightful to believe that the Spirit of God is the author of the great wave of prayer now breaking over our denomination's churches. It was not of our devising or planning, but it was the motion of God's Holy Spirit upon a few believers who desired to spend a day in honest prayer and found such a blessing they had to tell others. That movement spontaneously moved others, and without a word of objection or difference of opinion, all said, "Amen. Let us meet together for prayer also." The spirit of brotherly kindness and love was given, and then a spirit of earnest desire to bring down a blessing from God. It has not always been so. We have known the time when a day of fasting and prayer, if not despised, at any rate, would not have been appreciated. It has been a time where it seems as if it were the very breath of believers to breathe out longing desires for the revival of saints and the ingathering of sinners.

God is delighted to do great things in answer to our praying in the Spirit. Will you draw back now? Will you remain lukewarm in prayer? What! Do you have nothing to pray for? No children that concern your heart, no unsaved friends, no neighbors still in darkness? Where do you live! Is it in some vast wilderness where rumor of sin and ignorance has never reached your ear? Millions, millions despise the God who made them, despise the gospel of Christ—hear that word and see if you can tell its meaning. *Millions* are living without God and without hope and are going down to hell.

You are assailed by the wolf and the lion, the serpent and the bear. All forms of mischief are coming forth to attack the church. Not pray! If you are a Christian, you can pray—you must pray. Poverty does not make you poor in prayer, lack of education need not hinder you upon your knees, position and rank in society will be no incumbrance to you when you deal with God, who hears the poor man when he cries and answers him with a bounty of grace. It was when they were all met together with one accord in one place that suddenly they heard the sound as of a rushing mighty wind. We cannot be all in one place, but at any rate, let us be all with one accord.

If you love Christ, if you ever felt His love shed abroad in your heart and have been washed in His blood, I might put it to you as a demand, but I press it upon you as a brotherly entreaty: learn the secret of praying in the Holy Ghost. The Spirit has come. Beware of refusing His presence and finding the sweetness of devotion to have departed. He has not said to the seed of Jacob, "Seek ye my face in vain." Be hopeful, but do let us unanimously join in praying in the Holy Ghost.